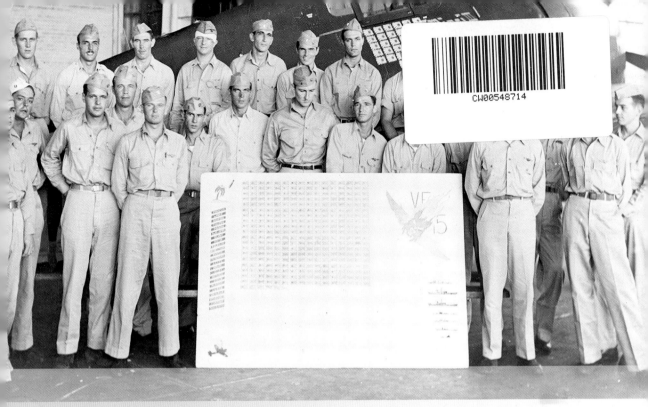

DOGFIGHT 5

F6F Hellcat
Philippines 1944

Edward M. Young

OSPREY PUBLISHING
Bloomsbury Publishing Plc
Kemp House, Chawley Park, Cumnor Hill, Oxford, OX2 9PH, UK
29 Earlsfort Terrace, Dublin 2, Ireland
1385 Broadway, 5th Floor, New York, NY 10018, USA
E-mail; info@ospreypublishing.com
www.ospreypublishing.com

OSPREY is a trademark of Osprey Publishing Ltd

First published in Great Britain in 2022

© Osprey Publishing Ltd, 2022

ISBN: PB 9781472850560; eBook 9781472850577; ePDF 9781472850584;
XML 9781472850553

22 23 24 25 25   10 9 8 7 6 5 4 3 2 1

Edited by Tony Holmes
Cover and battlescene artwork by Gareth Hector
Ribbon and tactical diagrams by Tim Brown
Armament artwork by Jim Laurier
Maps by www.bounford.com
Index by Fionbar Lyons
Printed and bound in India by Replika Press Private Ltd

Osprey Publishing supports the Woodland
Trust, the UK's leading woodland conservation
charity.

To find out more about our authors and
books visit www.ospreypublishing.com. Here you will find extracts, author
interviews, details of forthcoming events and the option to sign up for our
newsletter.

Front Cover Artwork: On September 13, 1944, Task Force 38 sent out
a fighter sweep followed by strike forces in a second day of attacks against
Japanese airfields on Negros and Cebu, in the Visayas. The Ki-43 "Oscars"
of 30th and 31st Sentai intercepted the American force, but in the battles
that followed lost between 16 and 20 aircraft. High-scoring Hellcat squadron
for the day was VF-31 flying off USS *Cabot* (CVL-28), whose eight pilots
claimed 19 "Oscars" in a fierce battle over Negros. The Ki-43s dove on the
VF-31 formation, which was escorting SB2C Helldivers and TBM Avengers,
from above and behind, but could not maintain their advantage. The Hellcat
pilots fought off the attack, and several subsequently attacked more "Oscars"
scrambled from Fabrica airfield below. Lt(jg) Arthur Hawkins was credited
with five victories and Lt James Stewart downed four, with three other pilots
claiming three apiece. (Cover artwork by Gareth Hector)

Previous Page: VF-15 pilots pose in the hangar bay of USS *Essex* (CV-9) on
December 1, 1944 at the end of a highly successful six-month deployment in
the western Pacific. Each of these Naval Aviators had been credited with the
destruction of five or more Japanese aircraft during the course of the cruise,
with Cdr David McCampbell, standing second from right in the front row,
leading the way with 34 victories. The commander of CAG-15, he flew the
F6F-5 serving as the backdrop to this historic photograph. (NHHC NH
106328)

Acknowledgments – I would like to acknowledge the invaluable work
done by the recently deceased Frank Olynyk in compiling his list of US
Navy claims for Japanese aircraft during World War II. Frank's prodigious
research served as a guide for this volume. I would again like to thank Holly
Reed and her able staff in the Still Pictures Branch at the National Archives
and Records Administration and Hill Goodspeed and his volunteers at the
National Museum of Naval Aviation. My good friend Osamu Tagaya shared
his extensive knowledge of Japanese military aviation in World War II. It
has been a pleasure to work with artists Tim Brown, Gareth Hector and Jim
Laurier during the compilation of this volume. I appreciate and admire their
ability to transform my ideas into dramatic images. Thanks also to my editor,
Tony Holmes, for his continued interest in exploring US Naval Aviation in
World War II.

Contents

CHAPTER 1
IN BATTLE

In the early morning of September 12, 1944, the carriers of Task Force (TF) 38 prepared to launch aircraft for an attack on the Japanese airfields on the islands of Cebu and Negros, in the Visayas in the Central Philippines. TF 38's mission was to put maximum pressure on Japanese air forces in the Philippines in support of landings on the islands of Peleliu and Morotai, scheduled for September 15.

On September 9, TF 38's aircraft had carried out strikes against Japanese shipping and airfields on the island of Mindanao, in the southern Philippines, meeting little in the way of aerial opposition. This day would be different. The Hellcat pilots would run into determined opposition from Imperial Japanese Naval Air Force (IJNAF) and Imperial Japanese Army Air Force (IJAAF) fighters in numbers they had not encountered since late July during attacks on Iwo Jima. The pilots would claim 82 Japanese aircraft shot down, with an additional 11 probably shot down and 16 damaged, as well as more destroyed on the ground.

The morning's attacks began with a fighter sweep by eight Hellcats from VF-19 off USS *Lexington* (CV-16) and eight from VF-15 off USS *Essex* (CV-9) over the airfield on central Cebu and Opon airfield on Mactan Island off the Cebu coast. VF-19, leading the sweep, remained as high cover over the Cebu airfield, while VF-15's two divisions went down through the thin overcast to scout the target area. Diving down, Lt Cdr John Rigg, CO of VF-15, saw many aircraft on the airfield apparently ready to take off. A rumor of an American landing on Mindanao had drawn 89 Zero-sens from 201st Kokutai down to the Cebu airfields from Manila. About half this force remained on Cebu, preparing to return to Manila once it had been determined that no such landing had taken place. These aircraft were on the cusp of taking off when the American fighter sweep came in.

Rigg ordered his two divisions to strafe the fighters on the field below. Ens Larry Self was flying on the mission that day with his section leader Lt(jg) William Henning. Self had received his commission as a Naval Aviator in December 1943 and had joined VF-15 in May 1944. He had yet to make a claim for a Japanese aircraft. VF-15's Aircraft Action Report described Self's first aerial victories after months of combat:

> Ens Self, after numerous strafing runs, saw a Zeke on Ens Brex's tail and turned, climbing, to get a full deflection burst into the Zeke's engine and cockpit. The Zeke broke up in mid-air and the parts scattered onto the field in flames. Ens Self's section leader [Lt(jg) Henning] sighted a Zeke climbing towards the West. Self and Henning immediately started a climb and soon made a tail run on the Zeke, which turned, heading for Self. When the Zeke had nearly closed and was a little down, Self dipped his nose and got a burst into the Zeke, from which it burst into flames, and Self pulled up. As he did so, Henning slid underneath (toward the flaming Zeke), and at that instant a large explosion threw Self high up in the air. Self whipped around and saw parts of an aircraft falling, with much smoke, but never saw Henning again (who is missing in action). Self then looked for a friendly VF and joined up on Lt(jg) Carr, and together with him caught an Oscar with a full deflection shot coming out of a loop, the Oscar bursting into flames and the pilot bailing out.

Three F6F-5s of VF-15 on board USS *Essex* (CV-9), with an older F6F-3 just visible on the right, in October 1944. This unit claimed 58 Japanese aircraft shot down during the September 12–13, 1944 strikes in the Visayas. Squadron CO Lt Cdr John Rigg led the way with five victory claims on the 12th. (80G-158174, RG80, NARA)

Later that morning, Lt William Knight led two divisions from VF-14, flying off USS *Wasp* (CV-18), as escort to two divisions from VB-14 and two divisions from VT-14 to attack the airfields on Negros Island, west of Cebu. Knight had begun his training in 1941 and received his commission as a Naval Aviator in 1942, serving as an instructor prior to joining VF-14. He had more combat experience than Ens Self, having claimed a "Kate" shot down and a half share in a "Tony" during the Marianas Turkey Shoot on June 19. The Hellcats ran into "Oscar" fighters from 30th and 31st Sentai who put up a strong resistance, as recorded in VF-14's Aircraft Action Report:

> Enemy planes in today's combat pressed home their attacks more vigorously than any this squadron has yet encountered. In spite of the general melee, these Japs attacked very effectively, jumping our formation from above and out of the sun, using high-side, overhead and head-on passes. They pulled tight turns to make our deflection shots more difficult. They always attempted to get on our tails, and would dive down, level off sharply and then outclimb the F6Fs. Their greatest weakness seemed to be gunnery, as not a single one of our planes received a bullet hole.

Knight's own account of the combat illustrates how the Hellcat pilots used their training, teamwork and discipline to claim six Japanese aircraft destroyed and five damaged after escorting the bombers during their attack runs. At the rendezvous point two pilots from his divisions shot down a "Nick," and shortly thereafter they became involved in an on-going combat between F6Fs and Japanese fighters. Knight subsequently recounted in his Aircraft Action Report:

The aces of VF-14 stand next to one of the squadron's F6F-3 Hellcats on board USS *Wasp* (CV-18) on November 1, 1944. Squatting at far left is Lt William Knight, who was the high scorer in the squadron with 7.5 victories and three damaged claims. He was listed as missing in action four days after this photograph was taken, having failed to return from a mission over the Clark Field area. Knight had shared in the destruction of two "Zekes" minutes prior to being shot down. (80G-349855, RG80, NARA)

I tally-hoed and led my division in to attack. As we attacked, the Jap planes rolled over and dived out. We maintained our altitude, circling to port, and were opened up on from above by about six more planes. A general melee followed. Three or four times I shot planes off of other F6Fs' tails, damaging one of them badly in the wingroot, as well as securing hits on the tails of two others.

Two or three times while making runs on Oscars about 2 o'clock from them, they turned head-on into me when I didn't think they could turn that sharply. It was one of these that came head-on that I smoked. He passed under me and rolled – a few seconds later I saw him splash. I observed 20mm fire from what was probably a Hamp (but might have been an Oscar) at a range of 200–300ft dead ahead, but luckily he missed me. On another occasion when Lt.(jg) Taylor, my wingman, and I were about 100ft apart, one of the Japs went under me and above Taylor. During one of these head-on attacks Taylor smoked a plane.

With Ens D. M. Gruber's section acting as my second section, we had a well organized division and we stuck together, never following the Jap planes down when they rolled and dived out. There were two *Hornet* planes that followed the Japs down past some clouds. My division shot Jap planes off their tails several times.

Knight claimed one "Oscar" destroyed and three damaged, while his wingman Lt(jg) Taylor was credited with two "Hamps" (most likely "Oscars" as well) shot down and two more damaged. Other pilots in the division added an additional "Hamp" and a "Nate," adding to the "Nick" claimed earlier.

Self and Knight saw more combat the next day (September 13), with the former being part of the early morning fighter sweep led by high-scoring ace Cdr David McCampbell, commanding Carrier Air Group (CAG) 15. He led 24 Hellcats from VF-15 and VF-12 on a sweep over the Japanese airfields on Cebu and Negros before the strike force came in. Self was flying in Ens Wendell Van Twelves' section. Twelves had also completed his training in 1943 and joined VF-15 in May, claiming two "Zekes" shot down over the Marianas. By great good fortune, VF-15 ran into 22 Ki-27 "Nates" of the training unit 32nd Kyoiku Hikotai on a flight over Bacolod airfield on Negros. The VF-15 pilots attacked the formation, claiming 13 "Nates" shot down and three more as probables – a total close to the 12 aircraft lost by 32nd Kyoiku Hikotai that morning. In a running fight, Twelves and Self claimed three "Nates." VF-15's Aircraft Action Report noted:

Ens Self was flying with Ens Twelves, and together they had a field day, and seemed to spend a valuable part of their time shooting Nates off each other's tails. Self's first Nate was acquired that way from a bracket, getting into a 6 o'clock up position, catching the Nate unawares. Bursts went into the cockpit, and evidently got the pilot, because the plane didn't flame but broke off and into an ever-tightening spin, with no evident attempt to recover. It crashed just north of Bacolod field (1 Nate).

Self then saw a four-plane division of Nates break up directly above four F6Fs, while Twelves and Self were behind about 1,000ft. As the Nates attacked, it was only necessary to get on their tails, fire and confirm. Self picked one off an F6F's tail from

6 o'clock level with two short bursts and saw it catch fire and crash between some houses northeast of Bacolod field (1 Nate).

Self started to rejoin his section leader, who was following a Nate and being followed by another. Self got on the latter's tail, and as the Nate saw him and started to turn into a deflection, Self's bursts hit him in the cockpit, and although the plane didn't flame, it crashed southeast of Bacolod field (1 Nate). Shortly after this encounter, the sky ran out of Nates.

Ens Self had claimed 5.5 Japanese fighters destroyed, making him an ace in just two combats. He would go on to claim three more victories during the Philippines campaign.

That same morning Lt William Knight of VF-14 was escorting Lt Norman Kellogg, who was flying an F6F-3P photo-reconnaissance Hellcat, on a post-strike photo mission mounted in the wake of CAG-14's attacks on Negros. He and Kellogg encountered two determined Japanese fighters, Knight claiming an "Oscar" and a "Tojo" destroyed in the combats that ensued, as he recounted in the squadron's Aircraft Action Report:

At 0845 to 0850 Kellogg was flying north at about 4,000ft and I was escorting while he took his pictures. I spotted a lone Oscar about three miles away and just out of the sun – about 2 o'clock. I tally-hoed him and he came in on a head-on run. I pulled up slightly to take him head-on. This Jap was either the most determined or the damndest fool I had encountered. My bullets must have gone just over his head. He was firing all the way in. When it seemed we were about to crash, he dropped his starboard wing and I raised my starboard wing – we didn't miss by more than three to five feet! I pulled up and turned to port. I estimated the Jap's speed at 270–300 knots, while mine was 160–170 knots.

In the fight which ensued I had shots from above and astern at 7 to 9 o'clock. Kellogg was also making some runs on the plane. We forced him down to 200–300ft. One time I overshot while Kellogg was firing at him. When I pulled up and to the left the Jap had pulled up and almost collided with me.

Bacolod airfield, on the island of Negros, comes under attack on October 24, 1944, the US Navy Hellcat fighters strafing the base having set at least two Japanese aircraft on fire. This was one of the airfields that had been previously hit during TF 38's sweeps of Negros and Cebu, in the Visayas, on September 12–13, 1944. (80G-291235, RG80, NARA)

An F6F-5 of VF-31 lands aboard USS *Cabot* (CVL-28). At this time the Hellcat squadrons embarked in Essex-class fleet carriers and Independence-class light carriers were converting to the F6F-5 model of the Hellcat, although the F6F-3 continued to serve in decreasing numbers during the Philippines campaign. (80G-263244, RG80, NARA)

My final run was made after we had damaged the plane and he was low on the water – 75–100ft – still making turns. I hit him in the cockpit and wing roots from about 8 o'clock at a distance of 300ft and slightly above, and he burst into flames. He hit the water flat and skipped about 150 yards. The next time he hit the water he exploded. I made a quick turn and took a picture from 100ft with my K-25 camera before the wreckage could sink. Time 0855 hrs.

Kellogg started taking pictures again with me escorting going north again at about 3,000ft. Another lone plane came from the northeast and flew almost over us. I had tally-hoed him about two miles away. I thought the plane was an Oscar, but when Kellogg and I discussed this plane later, he said it was a Tojo. This plane was about 3,000ft above us and swung into position about 5 o'clock from us. We were in a defensive position about 150 yards apart when he started his run – a 50-degree high-side. I believe Kellogg was still taking pictures. Anyway, he dived on Kellogg and I pulled up to starboard, speed about 160–170 knots, and took a shot at him.

I lost speed considerably and fell off on my left wing. The Jap pulled up to port out of his run and got on my tail. I made a quick turn toward Kellogg and he made a run on the Jap from about 10 o'clock and the Jap rolled out and down. Soon after, I got a good burst into him from above with both of us in a dive. He went right down to the ground and leveled off – I pulled myself back in trying to level off before he did. Kellogg followed with a shot, but neither of us seemed to be very effective. I believe I was hitting him but not in a vital spot. My final run was made from 9 o'clock, slightly above, with the Jap at about 200ft. He flamed and dived into the ground and exploded just off the edge of one of their fields. I kicked around and took a picture of him burning from 200ft. Time 0907 hrs.

This was Knight's third success in two days. He would go on to claim two "Zekes" destroyed over Formosa on October 15 and share in the destruction of two more over Clark Field on November 5, only to be shot down and killed on the latter date.

Also flying a mission that morning (September 13) was Lt(jg) Cornelius Nooy of VF-31, embarked in the light carrier USS *Cabot* (CVL-28). Nooy was another Naval Aviator commissioned in 1943, although he had been serving with VF-31 since January 1944. He was already an ace, having claimed seven Japanese aircraft shot down prior to the September battles over Negros. That morning, eight VF-31 F6Fs escorted four VT-31 TBM Avengers on a strike of the airfields on northern Negros, in company with a force from CAG-8 off USS *Bunker Hill* (CV-17). Nooy was leading the second section in Lt Adolph Mencin's division escorting the TBMs.

Just before reaching their target, a large group of "Oscars" bounced the naval aircraft from above and behind. Nooy and his wingman, Ens Edward Toaspern, turned into the attack, and although out of range they began firing, turning the "Oscars" away from the TBMs. As Nooy and Toaspern pushed over to follow the TBMs down in their attack, they ran into a melee at 5,000ft. VF-31's Aircraft Action Report summarized what happened next:

NOOY fired snap shots at several bandits with unobserved results and finally settled on the tail of an Oscar. He closed rapidly, scoring good hits from 9–6 o'clock, and the Oscar burst into flames. Continuing the fight, NOOY's section got frequent head-on and full deflection shots while the Oscars turned into them for evasive action. Sighting two Oscars dead ahead, NOOY and TOASPERN gave chase. The Oscars broke in opposite directions; NOOY followed one and TOASPERN the

0810 hrs, SEPTEMBER 13, 1944

LEGASPI AIRFIELD, SOUTH LUZON

1 Lt Harrell H. Scales, leading eight F6F Hellcats from VF-31 (with three from VF-8 providing top cover) on a fighter sweep over south Luzon at 15,000ft, spots IJNAF fighters taking off from Legaspi airfield. He orders the VF-8 fighters to remain as top cover and then leads his two divisions down. Note that the aircraft numbers worn by the Hellcats in all of the diagrams within this book are representative, and not the actual numbers of the aircraft participating in the missions depicted in artwork. US Navy pilots typically recorded the unique Bureau of Aeronautics number of the aircraft they flew, but not the fighter's individual single or two-digit fuselage/tail number.

2 Scales and his wingman, Lt(jg) Samuel W. Godsey, pull in behind what they believe are three Ki-44 "Tojos" – they were probably A6M5 Zero-sens that had rendezvoused south of the airfield.

3 Coming in from astern, Scales shoots down one Zero-sen, seeing his bullets hit the engine and cockpit. Godsey pulls off slightly to one side and fires on a second Zero-sen, registering hits in its starboard wing and fuselage.

4 The third Zero-sen makes off and starts circling at low level. Lt(jg) James M. Bowie drops down to join Scales and Godsey chasing this aircraft in a circling combat, but none of the Hellcats is able to gain position.

5 Scales turns tightly to starboard and reverses course to come at the Zero-sen head on.

6 Scales fires at the rapidly closing Zero-sen, hitting it in the cockpit and wing roots. With the pilot incapacitated, the now burning fighter hits the ground and cartwheels into a line of palm trees.

other. Closing to a position 9–7 o'clock above, NOOY made consistent hits in the engine of the Oscar. NOOY described the kill as follows:

"I noticed a sudden loss of speed by the Jap plane; and barely missing the Oscar, I pulled up in a wing-over and saw that his engine was dead. The pilot had his goggles up and the hatch open and watched me go by with open mouth. As I lost speed I turned in and fired again while he tried a crash landing at high speed in a cultivated field. He hit the deck and his engine was torn loose and the fuselage broke aft of the cockpit. The plane then hit a ditch and was cart-wheeling and smoking as I went by."

An unidentified F6F joined NOOY and they attacked a couple of Oscars that escaped by split-S'ing. NOOY's report continues:

"With the F6F still on my wing, I attacked another Oscar low on the deck from 5–7 o'clock above, scoring hits in his wings and cockpit, but with no results. I pulled off to let another F6F try his luck, which was also bad. He broke off and I again dropped into the tail spot. The F6F made a 180° turn and left. If I had attempted to follow, the Oscar could have easily chandelled onto my tail. I got out one more good burst and all six gun barrels burned out. The Oscar was badly damaged but still flying. I thought of chewing his tail off with my prop but finally decided to try forcing him into the deck. As I pulled up over his plane, I noticed a rise in elevation and held my altitude to 50ft, with my right wing slightly down. I throttled back so he couldn't ease out. I just missed the treetops, and pulled up sharply to observe the Oscar piled into the hillside burning rapidly."

Lt(jg) Cornelius Nooy (standing to attention in the center of the photograph) of VF-31 is awarded the Distinguished Flying Cross on the flightdeck of *Cabot* on September 5, 1944 for previous combat action. He received his second Navy Cross for shooting down five aircraft in the first strike on the Manila area on September 21. Nooy would end the war with 19 victory claims against Japanese aircraft, earning him three Navy Crosses and two Silver Stars. (80G-263308, RG80, NARA)

Meanwhile, Toaspern had been involved in his own combats, claiming two "Oscars" shot down and two more damaged for his first victories since joining VF-31 earlier in the year. He would go on to claim three more Japanese fighters over the Philippines and two "Zekes" on the last day of the war. Nooy would be credited with the destruction of five fighters over the Clark Field area on September 21, and four more in July 1945, ending the war tied with Lt Patrick Fleming as the US Navy's fourth highest-scoring ace.

The combats of these five Naval Aviators on September 12–13, 1944 are representative of the experiences of the many Hellcat pilots who participated in the Philippines campaign between September 1944 and January 1945. The vigorous Japanese defense of the Philippines created many opportunities for new and experienced US Navy pilots to begin or add to their claims against enemy aircraft. There were days of intensive air combat. Of the US Navy's ten highest total daily claims in World War II, four occurred during the Philippines campaign. In the air battles over the Philippines and Formosa some 650 Hellcat pilots claimed one or more victories. Approximately 91 pilots claimed five or more victories, with 21 pilots claiming five or more victories in a single day – more than in any of the US Navy's other aerial battles.

Some pilots, like Lt(jg) Cornelius Nooy, added significantly to their prior claims to join the ranks of the US Navy's leading Hellcat aces, while others, like Lt Cecil Harris and Lt(jg) Douglas Baker, rose rapidly into these ranks with their victories in the Philippines campaign. The vast majority of Hellcat pilots, however, claimed just a few Japanese aircraft, many pilots making their only wartime claims during a single combat mission. Some 268 pilots claimed between one and two aircraft in combat, 160 claimed between two and three aircraft, 94 claimed between three and four, and 42 claimed between four and five aircraft, just missing out on the coveted title of ace. Each of these victories contributed to the destruction of Japanese air power over the Philippines and represented hundreds of hours of flying, not just on fighter sweeps or fighter escorts, but hours spent on combat air patrols (CAPs) or escorting SB2C Helldivers on long-range search missions.

In light of these successes against Japanese aircraft during the campaign, what is interesting is the relative lack of prior combat experience of many of the Hellcat squadrons and pilots that participated in the aerial battles. Of the 24 F6F-equipped squadrons that flew as part of TF 38 during the period, nine had no combat experience during 1944 prior to the Philippines campaign, while two squadrons had made just two claims for Japanese aircraft and a further five squadrons had 25 claims or less. Of the approximately 91 pilots credited with the destruction of five or more Japanese aircraft during the campaign, only 33 had made claims prior to the Philippine battles, and just nine had become aces in earlier aerial battles.

Ens Self and Toaspern made their first claims over Cebu and Negros on 12–13 September 1944, while Lt William Knight had been credited with just 1.5 victories before his combats on those dates. Their experiences were common. Their success is a testament to the training they received on the way to becoming Naval Aviators. Many of the American Hellcat pilots were just as inexperienced in aerial combat as their Japanese foes over the Philippines, but they had the benefit of better training and tactics, better marksmanship, more flying hours, and a superior aircraft in the F6F.

CHAPTER 2

SETTING THE SCENE

During the summer of 1944, American military planners in the Pacific and Washington, D.C. engaged in an intense debate over the next stage of operations against Japan. In June US forces had breached Japan's outer defense barrier. The US Navy's Fifth Fleet had defeated the Imperial Japanese Navy (IJN) in the Battle of the Philippine Sea and launched an invasion of Saipan in the Marianas, while in the Southwest Pacific Gen Douglas MacArthur's forces had captured Hollandia, in New Guinea, bypassing and isolating two Japanese armies.

Two operations were planned for September 1944 – the capture of the Palau Islands, in the western Pacific, to provide an anchorage for the US Navy's fleet, and Morotai in the Halmahera group, which would bring American air power within 300 miles of the Philippines. This was to be followed by a landing on Mindanao, in the Philippines, in November. The question before the American Joint Chiefs of Staff (JCS) was where to attack Japan after completing these operations.

Contrails over a carrier during the great Marianas Turkey Shoot on June 19, 1944. The loss of the Marianas was a critical blow to the Japanese, opening up their inner defense line to attack. (80G-236904, RG80, NARA)

The JCS continued to believe that Japan could only be defeated through an invasion of the Home Islands. Prior to this, US forces would have to break through Japan's inner defense barrier to establish a base for launching the invasion and to cut off the country's access to vital raw materials in Southeast Asia, particularly oil. The prospective targets were Luzon, in the Philippines, Formosa (as the Western powers called Taiwan at the time) and an area on the coast of China.

MacArthur, who was committed to liberating the Philippines, argued for invading Luzon and bypassing Formosa and the Chinese coast to advance to the Ryukyu Islands and subsequently a landing on Kyushu, in Japan. He proposed landing on Leyte, in the Philippines, in November, followed by an invasion of Luzon in March–April 1945. Adm Chester Nimitz, commanding US forces in the Central Pacific, preferred to bypass Luzon for a landing on Formosa, which was closer to the Home Islands, and then an advance to Japan. Both agreed, however, on the need for land-based aircraft to provide cover for further advances toward Japan, which required seizing areas for airfields along whichever route the JCS chose.

Nimitz came to agree with MacArthur's plan to capture Leyte as a base for aircraft, but still preferred to bypass Luzon in favor of Formosa. The JCS had earlier instructed MacArthur to plan for a landing on Luzon and for Nimitz to plan for an invasion of Formosa, but deferred a decision on which operation would go forward. Much depended on the resources that would be required for these operations, and what would be available in time. To succeed in this advance to Japan's inner defense line, US forces still needed to cripple the IJN fleet and significantly weaken Japan's air strength in the Philippines, Formosa and the Home Islands.

In late August, MacArthur proposed new target dates for his advance, with an initial landing on Mindanao on November 15, to be followed by a landing on Leyte on December 20 and Luzon in February 1945. By early September, it was becoming apparent that an invasion of Formosa would be a massive undertaking, and that the forces in the Pacific were inadequate for the task. Much would depend on the defeat of Germany and the release of American forces for the Pacific, but this now seemed unlikely to occur in time. Moreover, the Japanese *Ichi-Go* operation in China was eliminating the Fourteenth Air Force's bases in eastern China necessary for supporting any invasion of Formosa.

A famous photograph of the Fast Carrier Task Force, then designated TF 38 under Adm Halsey, at the Ulithi anchorage in December 1944 at the tail end of the Philippine campaign. From front to rear are the Essex-class carriers USS *Wasp* (CV-18), USS *Yorktown* (CV-10), USS *Hornet* (CV-12), USS *Hancock* (CV-19) and USS *Ticonderoga* (CV-14), whilst the fleet carrier painted in sea blue Measure 21 at upper left is their sister ship USS *Lexington* (CV-16). Two Independence-class light carriers can also be seen at anchor flanking *Lexington*. (80G-294131, RG80, NARA)

Gen George Marshall, US Army Chief of Staff, came to see an invasion of Luzon as likely to require fewer troops and result in fewer casualties. Adm William Leahy, Chief of the JCS, agreed, but suggested that the US Army and US Navy gather forces for either an invasion of Luzon or Formosa in 1945, and decide after reviewing results of the Leyte invasion. On September 8, with the US Navy's reluctant agreement, the JCS approved the landing on Leyte for December 20, followed by a planned landing on either Luzon or Formosa in February–March 1945.

Five days later Adm William Halsey, commanding Third Fleet, submitted a recommendation to advance the date of the Leyte invasion based on his perception of the weak Japanese response to the carrier strikes on Mindanao and the Visayas. Halsey did not believe it would take more than two months to reduce Japanese air strength in the Philippines and recommended abandoning the invasion of Mindanao in order to directly target Leyte. MacArthur and Nimitz agreed with Halsey's recommendation and forwarded the recommendation to the Allied Combined Chiefs of Staff (CCS) meeting in Quebec. The CCS apparently took just 90 minutes to agree, canceling the invasion of Mindanao and moving up the invasion of Leyte to October 20.

Because Leyte was beyond the range of MacArthur's Fifth Air Force fighters, the invasion would have to depend on the US Navy's carrier force to support the landing and negate the likely rapid reinforcement of Japanese air strength in the Philippines. To provide close air support for the landings, the US Navy's Seventh Fleet supporting MacArthur formed an escort carrier task group with 18 escort carriers equipped with F6F Hellcats, FM-2 Wildcats and TBM Avengers. The main striking force would continue to be Halsey's Third Fleet and its TF 38 Fast Carrier Force with the following complement of large Essex class carriers (CV) and smaller Independence class vessels (CVL):

TG 38.1 Task Group One
USS *Wasp* (CV-18) – CAG-1
USS *Hornet* (CV-12) – CAG-11
USS *Monterey* (CVL-26) – CAG-28
USS *Cowpens* (CVL-25) – CAG-22

TG 38.2 Task Group Two
USS *Intrepid* (CV-11) – CAG-18
USS *Hancock* (CV-19) – CAG-7
USS *Bunker Hill* (CV-17) – CAG-8
USS *Cabot* (CVL-28) – CAG-29
USS *Independence* (CVL-22) – Night Air Group 41

TG 38.3 Task Group Three
USS *Essex* (CV-9) – CAG-15
USS *Lexington* (CV-16) – CAG-19
USS *Princeton* (CVL-23) – CAG-27
USS *Langley* (CVL-27) – CAG-44

TG 38.4 Task Group Four
USS *Franklin* (CV-13) – CAG-13

USS *Enterprise* (CV-6) – CAG-20
USS *San Jacinto* (CVL-30) – CAG-5
USS *Belleau Wood* (CVL-24) – CAG-21

USS *Intrepid* (CV-11), the third Essex-class carrier commissioned, gathers speed in preparation for its next aircraft launch cycle in November 1944. During the Philippine campaign as many as nine Essex-class carriers were assigned to TF 38's three Task Groups. A Task Group normally consisted of two to three Essex-class carriers and two Independence-class light carriers (CVL). *Intrepid*, with CAG-18 embarked, was part of TG 38.2 during the fall of 1944. (NH 97468, Navy History and Heritage Command)

At that time, the normal complement of an Essex-class carrier air group was a fighter squadron (VF) with 36 to 48 F6F Hellcats, a bomber squadron (VB) with 25 to 30 SB2C Helldivers and a torpedo-bomber squadron (VT) with 18 TBM Avengers. The smaller Independence-class carriers carried 20 to 25 F6F Hellcats and nine TBM Avengers. This gave TF 38 a total force in excess of 1,000 aircraft, with more than half comprising of F6F Hellcats. It was the most powerful naval force ever assembled. At the start of the Philippine campaign, the Fast Carrier Task Force's fighter squadrons were transitioning from the F6F-3 to the F6F-5 Hellcat, so that the squadrons contained a mix of the two models, plus several F6F-3P and -5P photo-reconnaissance aircraft and a small contingent of F6F-3N or -5N nightfighters.

For Japan, MacArthur's capture of Hollandia, the defeat of the IJN in the Battle of the Philippine Sea and the loss of the Marianas were devastating blows. What the Imperial General Headquarters (IGH) had defined as Japan's "absolute" defense zone had been breached. The loss of Saipan forced Gen Hideko Tojo to resign as Prime Minister and Army Chief of Staff on July 22, 1944 and led to the IGH appointing new Army and Navy commanders.

The Independence-class light
carriers were a wartime
adaptation of Cleveland-class
light cruiser hulls to aircraft
carriers. The US Navy
completed nine ships of this
class during World War II. The
CVLs carried fewer aircraft than
the larger Essex-class carriers,
but all were completed during
1943, when they were badly
needed. Here, TG 38.3's USS
Langley (CVL-27), with CAG-44
embarked, leads USS
Ticonderoga (CV-14), three
battleships and four light
cruisers into Ulithi Atoll on
December 12, 1944 following
operations in the Philippines.
(80G-301354, RG80, NARA)

Japan's strategic situation was dire. America now had the initiative in the war, with a powerful fleet that could strike anywhere in the Pacific, new long-range B-29 bombers capable of reaching Japan from bases in the Marianas and submarines that were taking an increasing toll of merchant shipping bringing vital raw materials to Japan for its war industries. To compound Japan's problems, tens of thousands of soldiers, sailors and airmen, and thousands of tons of equipment, were now isolated on islands that the Americans had bypassed and could no longer play a part in Japan's defense.

The most critical threat to Japan was the potential loss of access to the resources of its conquests in Southeast Asia. Aircraft production would peak in October 1944 and never recover to the same level. New, more capable bombers and fighter aircraft were in production, but in numbers too limited to have a strategic impact. More importantly, shortages of fuel led to sharp cutbacks in pilot training. By the beginning of the Philippines campaign, the average IJNAF pilot had less than 400 hours of flying experience, while his counterpart in the IJAAF had less than 200 hours.

Japan now had to retreat to its inner defense line, stretching from the Home Islands to the Ryukyus, to Formosa and the Philippines and south to the Netherlands East Indies. The IGH developed plans for the defense of each of these regions under the designation *Sho-Go* (Victory). Operation *Sho No. 1* was for the defense of the Philippines, *Sho No. 2* for defense of Formosa and the Ryukyus, *Sho No. 3* defense of the Home Islands and *Sho No. 4* the defense of Hokkaido. When the Japanese military identified the target of American invasion, it would designate that area as the location for the decisive battle, activate the *Sho* attack plan and marshal all available air, sea and ground resources for the defense.

As Japanese planners considered how to defend this inner line and estimate the most likely target of American attacks, the Philippines quickly assumed paramount importance. Its loss would be catastrophic to the defense of the Empire. With control of the Philippines, US forces could cut the flow of raw materials vital to Japan's war effort, crippling the Empire. If Japan lost the Philippines, it would lose the war. Retaining the Philippines became the priority.

Over the summer of 1944 the Imperial Japanese Army and the IJN struggled to reinforce and strengthen the Philippines with additional air and ground forces, believing the Americans were unlikely to invade the region until November. The IJAAF's 4th Kokugun (Air Army), shattered in the battles over New Guinea, had retreated to the Philippines and took over responsibility for the IJAAF's contribution to its air defense. The IGH ordered the IJAAF's 2nd and 4th Hikoshidan (Air Division) to be transferred from Manchuria to the Philippines, with the former exercising control of operational units and the latter taking on administrative duties. By August, 2nd Hikoshidan had five Hikodan (Air Brigades) and one Sentai (Regiment) available, giving 4th Kokugun some 420 aircraft of all types deployed to the Clark Field area on Luzon and to Bacolod airfield on the island of Negros.

Among the units transferred at this time were 17th and 19th Sentai with Ki-61 "Tonys" to Manila to form the 22nd Hikodan, and 30th and 31st Sentai with Ki-43 "Oscars," which were sent to Negros to form 13th Hikodan. The IJAAF also sent twin-engined fighter, heavy and light bomber and reconnaissance

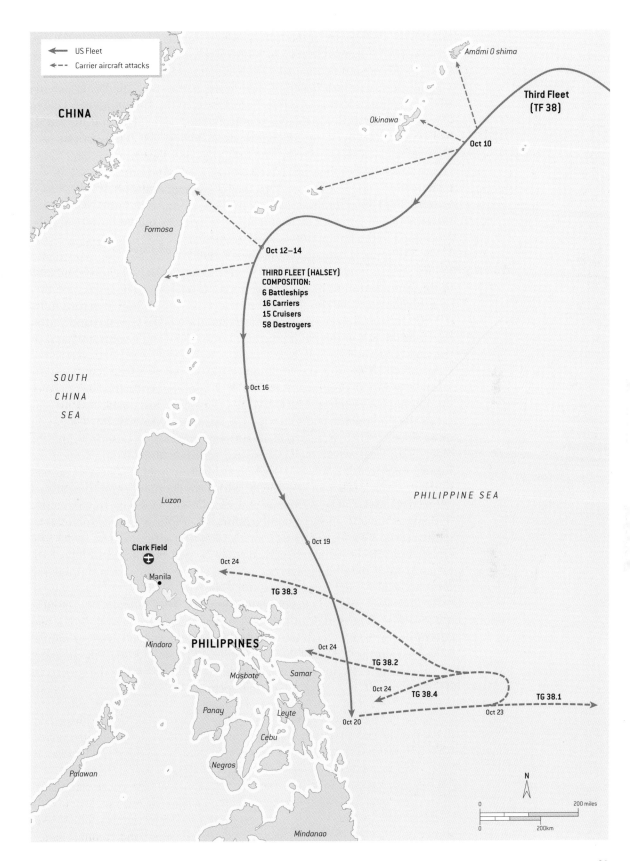

CHINA

Amami O shima

**Third Fleet
(TF 38)**

Okinawa

Oct 10

Legend:
→ US Fleet
⇠ - Carrier aircraft attacks

Formosa

Oct 12–14

THIRD FLEET (HALSEY)
COMPOSITION:
6 Battleships
16 Carriers
15 Cruisers
58 Destroyers

*SOUTH
CHINA
SEA*

Oct 16

PHILIPPINE SEA

Luzon

Clark Field
⊕

Manila

Oct 19

Oct 24

TG 38.3

Mindoro

PHILIPPINES

Oct 24

TG 38.2

Masbate

Samar

Oct 24

TG 38.4

TG 38.1

Panay

Leyte

Oct 23

Oct 20

Cebu

Negros

Palawan

N

0   200 miles

0   200km

Mindanao

units to the Philippines. If the IGH activated the *Sho No. 1* operational order, then the IJAAF planned to transfer more units from 8th Hikodan on Formosa, from 5th Kokugun in China and 3rd Kokugun in Southeast Asia.

Following its near destruction during the battles over the Marianas, the IJNAF's 1st Koku Kantai (Air Fleet) was moved to the Philippines, initially to Davao, on Mindanao, and then to Manila. By early September 1st Koku Kantai had around 400 aircraft of different types, including 210 Zero-sen fighters of 201st Kokutai, J1N1-S "Irving" nightfighters of 153rd Kokutai, and G4M "Betty" medium bombers of 761st Kokutai. 1st Koku Kantai's weakness was pilot quality – in 201st Kokutai, less than 20 percent of the pilots were classed as excellent or good. In the event of activation of *Sho No. 1*, 2nd Koku Kantai, then training in Japan for deployment to the Ryukyus and Formosa, would be transferred to the Philippines as reinforcements.

The Philippines contains more than 7,000 islands, but the main island groups are Luzon in the north, the Visayas in the central area and Mindanao in the south. Luzon is the biggest island, some 40,500 square miles (105,000 square kilometers) in area. Mindanao is next in size at 36,680 square miles (95,000 square kilometers). The Visayas are made up of several islands, from Samar in the east in the Philippine Sea, Leyte, Cebu and Negros, to Panay in the west bordering the Sulu Sea.

For much of the war the Philippines had served as a base for supplying Japanese armies in Southeast Asia and in the Southwest Pacific, and a center for training IJAAF pilots. The IJAAF and the IJNAF had established airfields across the Philippines, and following the loss of the Marianas hurriedly built more airbases. There were two main airfield complexes on Luzon, around the older Clark Field, where the Japanese had added six airfields, and around the former American Nichols and Neilson fields near Manila. The Visayas was home to another dozen or so airfields, with a similar number on Mindanao.

The distance by air from Manila to Tacloban, on Leyte, was approximately 350 miles (563km), allowing rapid reinforcement from the airfields on Luzon to the central Visayas, or to attack an invasion fleet off-shore. The IJAAF and IJNAF units in-theater also benefited from the well-established air links back to Japan from the Philippines, to Formosa and then on to Kyushu, via the Ryukyus. Units could be moved rapidly along this chain.

Weather would also be a factor in the campaign. The Philippines experiences a wet season from June through to November, when rain and clouds can cover parts of the area, with the added risk of typhoons. On Leyte, the rainfall is heaviest during November and December. This would delay the building of airfields on Leyte for the Fifth Air Force's fighters, forcing the carriers of TF 38 to remain in combat longer than planned.

CHAPTER 3
PATH TO COMBAT

Many of the young Hellcat pilots who participated in the Philippines campaign had enlisted in the US Navy during 1942 following the attack on Pearl Harbor on December 7, 1941, receiving their commissions as Naval Aviators in 1943. They were participants in the US Navy's greatly enlarged training program built up during the early months of the war to produce 20,000 pilots a year who had the skills and training required for air combat flying aircraft from carriers, naval vessels or land bases. The US Navy sought to recruit physically fit young men between the ages of 18 and 26 who could also meet its educational standards, initially through having completed at least two years of college tuition. Many came into the US Navy through the V-5 Naval Aviation Cadet program, which provided a route to pilot training and a commission in the US Navy Reserve.

Initially, a young man selected for pilot training started down the path of becoming a Naval Aviator at one of the Civilian Pilot Training Program (CPTP) schools located around the US. The Government had established the CPTP before America's entry into the war to provide a pool of men with elementary flying training who could be called to the services in the event of war. Using the CPTP removed the need for the US Navy to establish the many elementary training schools that would have been required to produce the number of pilots it needed. CPTP training also served as a screening mechanism to eliminate trainees who were likely to fail the US Navy's pilot training program at a later stage.

During their 12 weeks at a CPTP school, trainees would receive 72 hours of ground instruction in the theory of flight, navigation, engines, meteorology and radio communications. Using small light aircraft with civilian instructors, the CPTP schools provided 17 hours of dual instruction and 18 hours of solo flying, covering basic flying skills, landings and take-offs, simple maneuvers and cross-country flights. At the end of 1942, the CPTP schools were designated War Training Schools. In early 1943, the US Navy introduced Flight

The US Navy stressed physical fitness throughout a Naval Aviator's training, as flying a fighter could be physically demanding. Through physical training cadets came to be in the best shape they had likely ever been in and became accustomed to working as part of a team through playing team sports. These cadets are seen undertaking pre-flight school training at Saint Mary's College in Moraga, California, in 1943. (80G-K-15770, RG80, NARA)

The flightline at NAS Corpus Christi, Texas, in early 1943. All aspiring Naval Aviators flew the N3N or N2S during the primary phase of their training. In these biplanes cadets learned basic flying skills prior to going solo, after which they were taught how to fly with precision. (80G-475212, RG80, NARA)

Preparatory Schools, where aviation cadets received 15 weeks of ground instruction and intensive physical training before moving on to a War Training School.

After completing elementary flight training, the aviation cadet went to a pre-flight school for 11 weeks of academic instruction and intensive physical conditioning. Here, he received more training in navigation, meteorology, Morse code, aircraft recognition and US Navy history and regulations. Physical training emphasized team sports, especially American football, to develop a sense of teamwork.

From pre-flight school, the cadet went to one of the 16 Primary Training Schools located around the country. Here, the program of ground instruction and physical training continued, but the goal of primary flight training was to teach the cadet safe flying habits and instill strict flying discipline. Cadets received 90 to 100 hours of dual and solo flying time on Naval Aircraft Factory N3N or Boeing N2S biplanes, going through six stages – A: primary dual, B: primary solo, C: advanced solo, D: final qualification, E: formation flying, and F: night flying. The advanced solo stage introduced the cadet to aerobatics, stressing precision, rapid coordination and the ability to control an aircraft at any attitude. By stage D, the cadet had learned basic

Cadets began their intermediate training on the Vultee SNV, a heavier and more powerful aircraft than the N3N or N2S. Here, a line of SNVs at a flying school in Florida in early 1942 waits for flying instruction to begin. (80G-11274, RG80, NARA)

flying skills, so the emphasis shifted to training him to become a military flyer. Regular check flights ensured that each cadet met required standards.

From primary school, the cadet advanced to 14 weeks of intermediate training, in two stages, basic and advanced. In the intermediate phase training, the goal was to produce a military flyer, ready and capable of moving on to service aircraft. In the first four weeks of intermediate training the cadet learned to fly the Vultee SNV, an all-metal monoplane with fixed landing gear that was heavier and more powerful than the N3N or N2S. After becoming thoroughly familiar with the SNV, the cadet was introduced to flying in the US Navy's standard four-aircraft division and the basics of instrument flying in the Link Trainer and then flying under the hood in the SNV with an instructor or fellow student. Ground training continued with more intensive instruction in navigation and meteorology, instrument flying, aircraft recognition and, for the first time, aerial gunnery and combat tactics.

Before moving on to the advanced stage of intermediary training, the cadet received an assignment to the specialized type of aircraft he would fly once he became a Naval Aviator. The selection was based on personal preference, grades in ground and flying instruction and the needs of the US Navy. Those students selected for fighters transitioned onto the North American SNJ, the most powerful aircraft the student had yet flown, and the first with retractable landing gear. With the SNJ, the cadet continued to receive instruction in formation, instrument and night flying, but now added practice carrier landings, basic combat maneuvers and aerial gunnery. Ground instruction continued with more advanced courses in meteorology, navigation, combat tactics, communication, fixed gunnery and aircraft recognition.

Throughout the war the US Navy placed great emphasis on aerial gunnery. Indeed, it was one of the few air arms in the world at that time to provide intensive training in deflection shooting – the art of shooting at an angle to an enemy aircraft's flightpath. The US Navy divided the military pilot's job into three parts: the ability to fly an aircraft proficiently, the ability to fly a mission to a target and return to base, and the ability to accomplish the mission. By this point in a cadet's training he had learned to fly his aircraft and could now navigate from point to point with precision, but as the US Navy stressed, all the flying and all the navigation was useless if the fighter pilot could not achieve his primary mission – the destruction of enemy aircraft.

Cadets selected for carrier aviation (fighters, dive- and torpedo-bombers) progressed to the North American SNJ to bring them a step closer to service aircraft. With the SNJ, cadets received their first training in aerial gunnery. (80G-475219, RG80, NARA)

Through lectures, a series of booklets on fixed gunnery and films, the cadet was introduced to the basic gunnery approaches used in deflection shooting: the high-side, flat-side, low-side and overhead pass. Skeet shooting with shotguns taught cadets the basics of deflection shooting, including how to lead a target. Cadets would practice these approaches over and over, using the SNJ's single 0.30-cal. machine gun to fire at a target sleeve towed by a fellow cadet in another SNJ. Each cadet's ammunition was dipped in a different color of paint so that they could identify their individual hits on the target sleeve.

After four months of intermediary training the cadet received his Wings of Gold and a commission as an Ensign in the US Navy or a 2nd Lieutenant in the US Marine Corps. The next stage was eight weeks of operational training – what some termed the "postgraduate school of Naval Aviation."

Jacksonville, Florida, was the headquarters for all Naval Aviation operational training, with several airfields across the state for specialized tuition by aircraft type. Here, the neophyte Naval Aviators prepared to join a fleet squadron. By this point a typical US Navy pilot had accumulated around 330 flying hours, and was well-versed in basic maneuvers. Operational training focused on introducing the pilot to service combat aircraft and learning how to use it as a weapon, turning military pilots into combat pilots. During operational training the students were organized into four-man divisions, as they would be once they joined a combat squadron. Typically, a veteran pilot with combat experience would serve as an instructor for seven student pilots, forming two divisions. During their training, pilots would rotate positions within their division, serving as division or section leaders and as wingmen.

The first of three phases of operational training involved familiarization with a service aircraft. For pilots who went through operational training in late 1942 and early 1943, this was the Brewster F2A or the Grumman F4F Wildcat. The combat squadrons had priority for the latest fighter types. Once a pilot was familiar with the aircraft, regular training would begin – formation flying, instrument and night flying, navigation exercises and practice carrier landings.

While a mission during primary and intermediary training might have had a single objective, during operational training sorties more phases of combat flying were progressively added to a single mission. A gunnery mission, for example, might be combined with a navigational exercise to rendezvous and fly with another formation, stretching the demands on the trainee pilot. To the greatest extent possible, missions were flown over water to familiarize the trainees with the environment that they would experience operating from a carrier.

Ground instruction continued with sessions in the Link Trainer and the Gun Airinstructor – a basic simulator for aerial gunnery.

After receiving their wings and a commission as Ensigns, Naval Aviators selected for fighter squadrons went through operational training on service aircraft, where they learned and practiced the skills they would need as carrier fighter pilots. Many pilots who went through operational training in 1942 and early 1943 trained on the Brewster F2A, which few liked to fly. This weathered example, based at NAS Miami, is being flown by Lt Cdr Joseph C. Clinton on August 2, 1942. Clinton, who eventually achieved the rank of Rear Admiral, led Hellcat-equipped VF-12 into combat from USS Saratoga (CV-3) in 1943–44. (80G-16053, RG80, NARA)

There was intensive training in aerial combat so that the trainee would develop a full understanding of tactics and be able to react instinctively to a combat situation, performing the right action at the right time, almost without thinking. Flying the fighter had to become automatic so that the pilot could concentrate on his most important task: shooting down enemy aircraft. One of the most important lessons gained during operational training was the effectiveness of teamwork. Having veteran pilots who could impart their own experiences of combat was invaluable.

The final stage of operational training was qualifying on a carrier. For weeks the trainees had practiced field carrier landings – landing on an airfield marked out as a carrier deck under the guidance of a Landing Signal Officer. After completing their operational training, the pilots went to Chicago to make the required eight landings and eight take-offs from the converted paddle-wheel passenger vessels USS *Wolverine* (IX-64) and USS *Sable* (IX-81) sailing in Lake Michigan or on an escort carrier in the Chesapeake Bay. Once qualified, the pilots went to their first squadrons, where their training continued.

A pilot closes on the flightdeck of the training carrier *Wolverine* in an SNJ under the watchful eye of the Landing Signal Officer in January 1943. Carrier qualification was the final stage of operational training. Many young fighter pilots went to Lake Michigan to make the required eight landings and take-offs from *Wolverine* or *Sable*. (80G-34356, RG80, NARA)

During 1943–44, the US Navy established many new carrier air groups to man the equally new Essex- and Independence-class aircraft carriers joining the fleet. The carrier air group's component squadrons – fighter, dive-bomber and torpedo-bomber – had to be brought to the peak of efficiency before deploying on a carrier for combat. The training regime was progressive, beginning with the individual pilot, then the division, then the full squadron and, finally, the carrier air group together once each squadron had reached a satisfactory level of performance.

The typical fighter squadron was organized into divisions of four aircraft, which was its basic tactical unit. Each division consisted of four pilots, with two spare pilots. The division leader was usually a combat-veteran Lieutenant returning for another tour. The pilots lived and trained together, learning to anticipate each other's moves and thus allowing them to fight together as a team.

For the pilots, the first task was to become thoroughly familiar with the aircraft they would be flying in combat. For newer pilots, as well as returning veterans, this would often be their first encounter with the F6F Hellcat. The training was rigorous and intensive, often seven days a week, with only a half-day off. As one new Hellcat pilot recalled, "after a while it seemed as though our airplanes were part of us, and flying was becoming as natural as a reflex."

They practiced field carrier landings and started gunnery training, with the pilots of the division taking turns towing a banner target in an SNJ. The older veterans trained the younger pilots in combat tactics, passing on what they had learned in combat with the Japanese. The pilots practiced combat tactics, bombing and strafing techniques, and their role as escorts to the dive- and torpedo-bombers. Those who could not meet the standards set were weeded out and sent to another assignment.

A group of F6F-3 Hellcats at NAS Whidbey Island, in Washington State, likely belonging to a fighter squadron working up in preparation for deployment to a carrier. After joining a squadron, the novice Naval Aviator continued intensive training in fighter tactics and gunnery prior to being deemed ready to engage the enemy. (National Museum of Naval Aviation)

Once all the carrier air group's squadrons had demonstrated their capability, practice missions for the entire carrier air group would begin. After four to five months of training, a carrier air group would be deemed ready to deploy to its assigned carrier. Once on board, training would continue until the vessel entered combat. By this point, a young Hellcat pilot would be capable of flying his aircraft with precision in combat, would be familiar with standard combat tactics and gunnery approaches and would have amassed many more flying hours than his average Japanese opponent.

Nearing the end of their exhaustive flight training, fresh-faced Naval Aviators pose with a well-used F6F-3 at NAS Vero Beach, in Florida, in 1944. More than 237,100 hours of military flying was logged at the former municipal airport between 1942 and 1946, many of them by would-be fighter pilots in F6Fs. (National Museum of Naval Aviation)

CHAPTER 4

WEAPON OF WAR

The pilots of VF-18 called the Hellcat the "fightingest damned plane in the Pacific." Legendary Royal Navy test pilot Capt Eric "Winkle" Brown rated the Hellcat the greatest single-seat carrier fighter of World War II. The F6F changed the course of the US Navy's war in the Pacific, giving American carriers a fighter that could, with the right tactics, best the IJNAF's vaunted A6M Zero-sen. The big Grumman fighter was never as maneuverable as the A6M, but it was faster in level flight, much faster in a dive and maneuverable enough to follow a Zero-sen part way through a turn, getting in a quick burst.

To escape an attack, a Hellcat pilot could dive away at high speed, jinking at speeds where the Zero-sen's controls stiffened up. The Hellcat's speed and diving attacks negated the Zero-sen's maneuverability, while a burst from its six 0.50-cal. machine guns was often enough to set the less well armored IJNAF fighter on fire. The Hellcat was rugged, being able to absorb a considerable amount of damage and still bring its pilot back to the carrier.

The Grumman XF6F-1 with the Wright R-2600 Cyclone 14 engine first flew on June 26, 1942. The R-2600 did not give the XF6F-1 the performance that Grumman and the US Navy were hoping for. (72-AC-21G-10, RG72, NARA)

Perhaps its greatest attribute was the relative ease of landing a Hellcat on a carrier. On the approach to the vessel the F6F had excellent visibility, and could be flown onto the deck with precision, while its strong landing gear could absorb the shock of a hard landing. For young pilots with only a few hundred hours' flying experience, this was a gift.

Fortuitously, the Hellcat arrived just as the new, large Essex-class carriers were coming into service, and as the US Navy found, to its disappointment, that the early versions of the Vought F4U Corsair were proving to be difficult to land on a carrier. Designed as a replacement for Grumman's F4F Wildcat, and as insurance against problems with the XF4U Corsair, the US Navy gave Grumman a contract for two prototype XF6F-1s on June 19, 1941. The XF6F-1 made its first flight just over a year later, on June 26, 1942 – a remarkable achievement.

Even more remarkably, at the US Navy's request, Grumman replaced the prototype's 1,700hp Wright R-2600 engine with the more powerful 2,000hp Pratt & Whitney R-2800 Double Wasp in a little less than two months. The XF6F-3 made its first flight on July 30, 1942, and the first production aircraft took to the air for the first time on October 3, 1942 – 16 months after the US Navy placed its order for the XF6F-1.

The F6F-3 was well-designed for quantity production. By June 1943, Grumman was turning out close to 200 Hellcats a month, and it reached a production rate of 500 a month in January 1945.

The heart of the Hellcat was Pratt & Whitney's R-2800 Double Wasp engine. This powerful and reliable 18-cylinder, radial air-cooled engine was built in prodigious quantities during the war, with Pratt & Whitney and its automotive company licensees completing 112,916 R-2800s.

The story of the R-2800 is, like the Hellcat, one of the right engine appearing at the right time. During the 1930s, Pratt & Whitney competed fiercely with the Wright Aeronautical Corporation. In the middle of the decade the company began to consider building a large, powerful engine to compete with Wright's then new 14-cylinder R-2600 Cyclone 14 that initially offered 1,600hp. In 1937, Pratt & Whitney started design work on a larger 18-cylinder engine that had the potential for reaching 2,000hp. At the time it took four to five years to get a high-performance engine from design into production. Pratt & Whitney went through three years of intensive testing of every component of the engine to ensure that they worked together in harmony. Limited production of the R-2800 began in 1939, in time to influence the design of the Corsair, the Republic P-47 Thunderbolt and the Martin B-26 Marauder, and to be available for the F6F Hellcat when the US Navy and Grumman realized the Wright R-2600 would not give the new fighter the performance required for frontline service.

Grumman rapidly adapted the XF6F-1 to take the more powerful 2,000hp Pratt & Whitney R-2800 Double Wasp radial. This rugged and dependable engine gave the Hellcat the performance it needed to establish a clear superiority over the IJNAF's A6M Zero-sen. Devoid of any armament, this early-build F6F-3 is being put through its paces during a service test flight in late 1942. (72-AC-21F-7, RG72, NARA)

The F6F-3 was powered by the R-2800-10, which had a gear-driven two-speed, two stage supercharger giving 2,000hp for take-off and 1,650hp at 22,000ft. With the R-2800-10, the F6F-3 had a top speed of 376mph (605km/h) at 20,000ft – some 25mph (40km/h) faster than the A6M5 model of the Zero-sen at the same altitude. The cockpit of the F6F was comfortable and well laid out, with good visibility over the nose for landing and aerial gunnery. In addition to its powerful armament, the F6F-3 had armor protection in front of and behind the pilot and surrounding the R-2800's oil tank and oil cooler.

Entering squadron service in January 1943, the F6F-3 scored its first victory over a Japanese aircraft on September 1, 1943 when two pilots from VF-6 shot down a Kawanishi H8K2 "Emily." Beginning with the first carrier strikes in the fall of 1943, and continuing in the Marianas Turkey Shoot of June 19–20, 1944, the Hellcat established its ascendency over the Zero-sen.

During April 1944, Grumman transitioned from manufacturing the F6F-3 to the F6F-5. The new model incorporated improvements based on experience with the early Hellcat variant in combat. Grumman changed the powerplant in the F6F-5 to the R-2800-10W, which used water injection to give an additional 200hp. A refined cowling design to smooth the airflow and a change to a highly polished glossy sea blue paint scheme helped increase the F6F-5's top speed to 380mph (610km/h).

The aircraft's ailerons were fitted with spring tabs to lighten the stick forces, and together with a stronger tail and horizontal stabilizer structure, this contributed to improved maneuverability. A revised windshield provided greater visibility for the pilot and increased armor protection. Two inboard wing stations were equipped to carry 1,000lb bombs and later models added six stations on the outboard wing for 5-in. High Velocity Aircraft Rockets, turning the Hellcat into an effective fighter-bomber.

The F6F-5 began reaching carrier squadrons in the summer of 1944. During the Philippines campaign the squadrons progressively exchanged their older F6F-3s for the new F6F-5s, flying a mix of both models on operations. By the end of the campaign the F6F-5 predominated.

The F6F-3 production line at Grumman's Bethpage, Long Island, factory in February 1943. The company completed just 35 Hellcats that month as production of the new fleet fighter slowly ramped up, and by December 1943 it had delivered 458 examples. Throughout 1944 Grumman was churning out an average of 500+ F6Fs per month. (NARA)

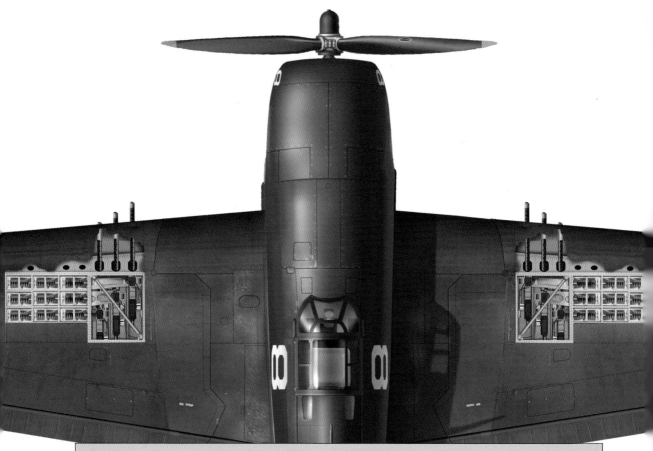

F6F-5 ARMAMENT

As with the F6F-3, the F6F-5 Hellcat was fitted with six 0.50-cal. Browning M2 machine guns in the outer wing sections, with 400 rounds per gun. The weapons were staggered to allow storage for the metal ammunition boxes containing the 0.50-cal. rounds, and to ease feeding the ammunition to the guns. The Browning M2 could fire at a rate of 600 to 850 rounds per minute, expending armor-piercing or armor-piercing-incendiary bullets. A burst of a few seconds was perfectly adequate to down the poorly protected mid-war IJAAF and IJNAF fighters and medium bombers, but better armored late-war Japanese fighters with self-sealing fuel tanks proved more difficult to destroy.

Grumman developed a revised armament installation for the F6F-5N nightfighter with one 20mm Hispano M2 cannon and two 0.50-cal. Browning M2s in each wing, but this was not adopted for the standard F6F-5 Hellcats equipping carrier-based fighter squadrons during 1944–45.

The normal complement for a Hellcat squadron on an Essex-class carrier was 36 aircraft. When the Japanese began launching kamikaze attacks against American carriers in October 1944, there was a desperate need for more fighters for CAPs, but this reduced the number of escorts available for strike aircraft. The immediate solution was to expand the fighter squadron complement to 50 or more Hellcats. In January 1945, the squadron complement was increased to 72 aircraft and 110 pilots, the number of SB2C dive-bombers being reduced to 15 aircraft to free up space for more fighters. When this became administratively unwieldy, the squadrons were divided into two, one nominally a pure fighter squadron (VF) and one a fighter-bomber squadron (VFB), often manned by former SB2C pilots.

As the Fast Carrier Task Force operations neared Japan, F4U Corsairs began to replace the Hellcat on board Essex-class carriers in both the VF and the VFB roles, with US Marine Corps Corsair squadrons flying off the vessels for the first time in the war.

The Hellcat instilled confidence in its young pilots. Lt William E. Davis, who flew Hellcats and earned the Navy Cross during the Philippines campaign, recorded his impressions of his first flight in a F6F in his post-war memoir *Sinking the Rising Sun*:

Revving up the engine and my nerves at the same time, I opened the throttle. The noise was fantastic. The response was instantaneous. Correcting for the torque of the giant engine, I started straight down the runway. I glanced at the instruments and couldn't believe I had only applied half the engine's power. I pushed the throttle against the stop – the surge of power and speed was incredible. The tail came up immediately as I eased the stick forward. A slight pull back and I was in the air. Crossing the field, I was already at 500ft. This thing really sang the song of the birds. I was really flying, and I had six 0.50-cal. machine guns, unloaded at the moment, but I knew I was ready for those Japs.

In April 1944 Grumman stopped building the F6F-3 and shifted to producing the more capable F6F-5, an early example of which is shown here during testing at NAS Patuxent River in May 1944. The F6F-5 added several refinements and a more powerful R-2800-10W engine with water injection. (80G-228822, RG80, NARA)

F6F production reached a peak in March 1945 when Grumman built 605 Hellcats at Bethpage. The final F6F-5 was rolled off the line in November 1945. These brand new F6F-5s are awaiting collection at the Long Island plant. (National Museum of Naval Aviation)

CHAPTER 5

ART OF WAR

The US Navy's carrier fleet doctrine specified that the primary mission of the fighter squadron was defensive, to protect its own forces, either ships at sea, shore installations or carrier strike forces, from enemy air attack. A fighter squadron's secondary mission was offensive, to attack enemy air, surface and ground forces through fighter sweeps and other attack missions. In both the defensive and offensive roles, the fighter pilot's objective was to destroy enemy aircraft. To achieve this objective, the US Navy had developed, and proved in combat, tactics that would enable a pilot to close with an enemy aircraft. He could then employ an effective system of aerial gunnery in the form of deflection shooting in order to maximize the chances of destroying the aircraft of his opponent. Success in air combat required "proper and thorough indoctrination, repeated combat practice and constant drill in the air . . ."

The US Navy had developed four basic principles for fighter combat:

- Superiority of Position
- Superiority of Disposition
- Superiority of Concentration
- Superiority of Marksmanship

The US Navy defined superiority of position as maintaining an altitude advantage against enemy aircraft and maintaining an "interior position" – a position that enemy aircraft would have to fly past in order to either press home an attack or to retreat from an engagement.

Superiority of disposition referred to the most efficient placement of fighter formations – sections, divisions or a full squadron – to accomplish their mission. Superiority of concentration reflected Carl von Clausewitz's maxim that the best strategy was to be very strong at the decisive point of battle. "There is no higher and simpler law of strategy," von Clausewitz wrote, "than that of keeping one's forces concentrated." The US Navy stressed over and over the necessity of teamwork in aerial combat and keeping together. The latter meant maintaining the ability to exercise leadership and protection in a general melee. Fighter sections and divisions had to stick together to provide mutual support. As the US Navy's statement of carrier tactics and doctrine explained, "each plane is part of an invisible chain. Any plane which breaks the chain by diving away either to avoid an enemy or in pursuit of a target, subtracts from the overall strength of the group." If the fighters maintained concentration, "they will command the air where they are concentrated."

Superiority of marksmanship comprised four basic principles:

- Ability to hit with the first burst of fire.
- Ability to make effective runs in the heat of battle on a maneuvering target.
- Cool selection of the point of aim – engine, pilot, or fuel tanks – rather than spraying the whole target.
- Conservation of ammunition.

The US Navy's offensive tactics were derived from these fundamental principles and encapsulated in a simple A-B-C formula:

US Navy fighter pilots were first taught the basics of air gunnery during the advanced phase of their intermediate training, using the 0.30-cal. machine gun in the SNJ to fire at a target sleeve towed by another SNJ. Each pilot's ammunition was dipped in a different color of paint. Here, cadets check the sleeve hoping to see their hits at NAS Corpus Christi. (80G-475244, RG80, NARA)

- A – Altitude advantage: gain and maintain it.
- B – Bracket the enemy and shoot from behind.
- C – Combat concentration: attack the enemy with more than one aircraft.

US Navy training drummed into fighter pilots the maxim that "Altitude is your wealth: never spend it unless it buys you speed or an advantageous firing position." The ideal was to attack an enemy aircraft with an altitude advantage, beginning the approach from 1,000ft above the target. The attacking fighter could make a gunnery pass, then break away and use the speed built up in the dive to climb back to altitude for a second attack.

Bracketing the target meant placing aircraft, sections or divisions abeam of each other above and ahead of the target so whichever direction the enemy aircraft turned, it would come under attack. If the enemy aircraft flew a straight course, individual fighters or sections could make simultaneous attacks from two directions. In bracketing the target the section would maneuver to get

behind the enemy aircraft to shoot it down. US Navy tactics were less concerned about which pilot or which section shot down an enemy aircraft and more concerned with shooting it down. "The whole idea," the US Navy's manual on tactics against enemy fighters stated, "is to gang up on the enemy, pitting two airplanes against his one, so that he has not a chance."

A B6N "Jill" torpedo-bomber comes under attack from an F6F during the October–November 1944 aerial battles over the Philippines. The US Navy trained its fighter pilots to maintain an altitude advantage over enemy aircraft and to aim for specific points, such as the wing fuel tanks, as shown here. This photograph was taken by the gun camera installed near the wing root of the port wing. It was operated when the pilot thumbed the trigger button on the control column. An "overrun control" kept the camera running from one to five seconds after the gun ceased firing. (80G-46983, RG80, NARA)

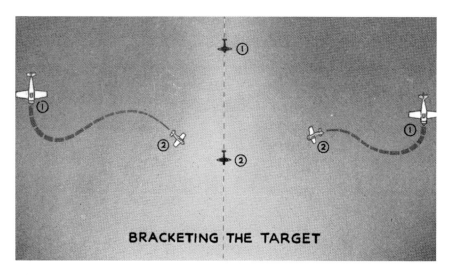

BRACKETING THE TARGET

The tactic of bracketing the enemy aircraft required and reinforced the need for combat concentration. The two aircraft in a section had to work together to defeat the enemy. In going into attack a pair of enemy fighters, US Navy pilots were trained to always target the fighter flying at the higher altitude first so as to avoid having to initiate an attack below an enemy fighter. The same rules and tactics applied to a division of four aircraft, working as a team to bracket the enemy, maneuvering to a position behind and maintaining concentration.

An important concept in the US Navy's doctrine for aerial combat was to bracket an enemy aircraft so that in whichever direction the pilot turned, he would come under the fire of one of the attacking fighters, or sections, as this diagram illustrates. (Author's Collection)

The objective of these combat tactics was to place a fighter, a section or a division in a favorable position to make an attack on an enemy aircraft. Through years of practice the US Navy had developed a system of gunnery approaches designed to give the attacking fighter the best chance of shooting down an enemy aircraft with the least risk. The US Navy warned young pilots to learn these approaches well:

- You can use them as a guide to ensure victory if you live up to them.
- You can disobey them only once, for they are enforced by adversaries who are quick to take advantage of any violation of them, whether willful or accidental.
- And the penalty is death.

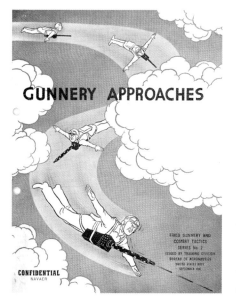

GUNNERY APPROACHES

FIXED GUNNERY AND
COMBAT TACTICS
SERIES No. 2
ISSUED BY TRAINING DIVISION
BUREAU OF AERONAUTICS
UNITED STATES NAVY
SEPTEMBER 1943

CONFIDENTIAL
NAVAER

The US Navy had four basic approaches: from the side, from overhead, from the stern and from head-on. Side approaches always began at an altitude above the enemy aircraft, with the fighter coming down in an "S" turn to attack the enemy aircraft from above, at the same level or from below, then breaking away safely to climb back up for another attack. The overhead approach also began several thousand feet above an enemy aircraft, and involved rolling in on the enemy to attack from above. The head-on attack was not often used, as it involved a rapid closing speed with little time to align and fire, and the risk of running directly into the enemy aircraft's return fire, but it could be employed in extremis. Stern attacks, too, had limitations. While suitable for attacking enemy fighters, a stern attack risked running into fire from an enemy bomber's guns.

The choice of gunnery approach depended on many variables: the type, number and speed of the enemy aircraft, weather conditions, the element of surprise and the fighter's own performance. And at times, it was necessary "to barrel on in and attack without gaining a favorable position." But, as the US Navy admonished its pilots, "there is no conceivable position for the initiation of an attack where the fundamentals of the [gunnery approaches] cannot be used." For this reason, Naval Aviators had to become expert in all gunnery approaches.

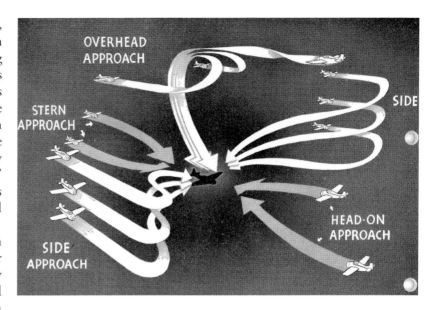

A diagram taken from the US Navy manual on offensive tactics against fighters showing the basic gunnery approaches. The US Navy combined these approaches with training in deflection shooting, teaching fighter pilots how to lead an aircraft and fire from different angles. Deflection shooting improved a pilot's chances of damaging an enemy aircraft. (Author's Collection)

As well as choosing an approach to the target, a fighter pilot had to simultaneously use what the US Navy termed the Who-Where-When system of fixed gunnery. "Who" referred to identifying an aircraft as friendly or enemy, and if the latter, then what type of aircraft? It was critical for a pilot to know the enemy aircraft's strengths and weakness – for example, the extent of armor protection and the location of the fuel tanks, as well as its speed. This was why training in aircraft recognition was so important.

"Where" referred to the aiming point, which depended on the enemy aircraft's speed and flight path. Pilots had to determine the correct amount of lead, or deflection, so that their bullets would reach a spot in space just as the enemy aircraft did so. Mastering the art of deflection shooting, through countless hours of practice, meant the US Navy pilot was not limited to an approach on the enemy aircraft from the stern, but could fire from different angles.

"When" referred to when to open fire. The US Navy recommended opening fire at a distance of 1,000ft from the target, and it taught pilots how to calculate range using the rings on the aircraft's ring gunsight. Becoming an expert in aerial fixed gunnery, knowing the gunnery approaches, estimating the amount of deflection and calculating the correct range at which to open fire required constant practice.

The US Navy developed doctrine for the principal missions (CAP, escort and offensive sweeps) of its fighter squadrons. The development of radar and fighter direction had greatly enhanced the ability of fighters to defend their carriers. Successful interceptions required the closest cooperation between the fighter director and the fighters on CAP, and effective teamwork among the sections and divisions.

Standard operating procedure was for a fighter squadron on a large carrier to assign 12 aircraft to CAPs, with 12 more remaining ready on the flightdeck. In multi-carrier groups one carrier could be assigned to provide its fighter squadron for patrol duties. There were three CAP stations – the patrol station orbiting the carriers in a circle up to ten miles in diameter at 10,000–12,000ft; the intercept station orbiting the carrier flying within the same circle but at 20,000ft; and the anti-torpedo station orbiting at 5,000ft in a circle of five miles in diameter.

OPPOSITE
The fundamental basis for US Navy air combat was a set of gunnery approaches that its fighter pilots practiced over and over until they became second nature. During the war the US Navy produced a series of manuals on fixed gunnery, reinforcing the basic principles with films, training devices and flying exercises. (Author's Collection)

Hellcats would fly in one of four formations, waiting for instructions from the fighter director. Tracking an incoming raid on radar, the fighter director would provide a vector and the altitude of the enemy aircraft to the CAP formations. When the flight leader sighted the enemy formation, he would confirm the sighting and his position before attacking, and identify the type and number of enemy aircraft ("Hawks" were dive-bombers, "Fishes" torpedo-bombers and "Rats" enemy fighter aircraft). The flight leader would then decide the best means of attack, concentrating on enemy dive- and torpedo-bombers.

While the principle of superiority of concentration still applied, CAP doctrine recognized that there would be times when this principle had to be violated in favor of immediate attack. If the torpedo-bombers were seen to be splitting up for individual attacks or the dive-bombers were about to push over into their dives, then "desperate measures are essential to save the task force, and consequently each fighter must pick an enemy plane and cut him down."

The objective of fighter escort missions was straightforward: to protect the dive- and torpedo-bombers on their way to the target and back to the carrier. With a squadron of 36 to 40 fighters on the large carriers, the requirements for CAP missions meant that around 16 fighters in four divisions would be available for escorting the strike force, flying in four positions. Doctrine specified that one division would provide close support, with sections split to fly on each side of the bomber formation around 500ft above.

The close cover position followed the same scheme, with sections flying 2,000ft above the bombers. The intermediate cover position flew at 4,000ft above the bombers, with the high cover position higher still – ideally, that would be above the altitude of intercepting enemy fighters. If enemy aircraft attacked the bomber formation, the fighters provided a layered defense, with the close support sections responding first, then the close cover sections joining if needed, followed by the intermediate cover sections. The leader of the high cover sections was admonished not to give up his altitude advantage unless absolutely necessary for the defense of the bombers. Following the attack on the objective, the fighter sections were to spread out to cover the bombers as they retired to the rendezvous point.

Carrier strike formations were increasingly using Hellcats offensively if there were no enemy fighters in the area. The new F6F-5s that were equipping the fighter squadrons could carry bombs and rockets to augment their machine guns. Approaching a target, such as an airfield or shipping, the fighters would break off to go down to bomb, rocket and strafe, the divisions flying in line-abreast with 1,000ft between aircraft. Divisions made separate attacks from different angles so as to crisscross the target.

It was important to turn away from the target quickly to get out of range of anti-aircraft fire and regain concentration. Ideally, no two aircraft, sections or divisions followed the same path over the target in order to confuse the anti-aircraft gunners. On fighter sweeps against enemy airfields, one or more divisions would go down to bomb and strafe the field, leaving one or more divisions as high cover, then reversing the roles after the first divisions had completed their runs.

The different types of fighter missions all had the same requirements – disciplined teamwork, mastery of the gunnery approaches and excellent marksmanship. Doctrine stressed the need to fight offensively. As a US Navy

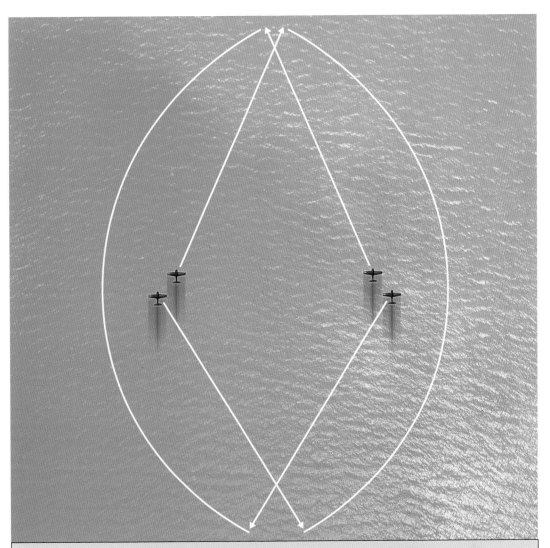

MUTUAL LOOKOUT RESPONSIBILITY DIAGRAM

The US Navy's fighter squadron formations were based on the two-aircraft section as the basic fighting unit and the four-aircraft division as the fighting team. The two-section division could maneuver easily, with sections flying abeam of one another and making simultaneous runs against an enemy aircraft to ensure they were in a position to provide mutual lookout and defense during all phases of the attack and recovery.

The division formation could quickly shift from the offensive bracketing tactic to the defensive beam formation as the situation dictated. Two sections spread apart and flying abeam provided good coverage from possible attack. The section to starboard would cover the approaches to the division on the port side, while the section to port would cover approaches to the starboard side, in a system the US Navy called "Mutual Lookout Responsibility".

manual stated, "the fighter pilot, whose primary mission is the destruction of enemy aircraft, doesn't belong on the defensive." Nevertheless, pilots had to learn to fight defensively if attacked, and particularly if separated from friendly fighters.

Pilots trained in the defensive formation that Lt Cdr John Thach had developed in 1942 to counter the Zero-sen's superior maneuverability. Initially dubbed the "Thach Weave" but now officially termed the Beam Defense, this involved two aircraft in a section or two sections in a division flying in line-abreast formation and turning towards each other if attacked. As the enemy aircraft attacked from astern, the aircraft or section under attack would immediately turn towards the other aircraft or section, which would immediately turn toward the attacking enemy aircraft to bring it under fire. By weaving continuously, a section could ward off continuous attacks. The benefit of the Beam Defense was that it mirrored the same formation used in bracketing enemy aircraft, so that a defense against attack could be quickly turned into an offensive attack.

There were, of course, situations where a fighter pilot might be caught entirely on his own. In this case US Navy training stressed countering an attack with a counterattack, turning defensive tactics into offense. The keys to a pilot's survival were knowing the capabilities of his own aircraft compared to his attacker, and having a plan of action thought out in advance. As the US Navy gunnery manual on defensive flying noted, when under attack "you haven't any time to work out tactical problems by higher mathematics when you have a Zero on your tail."

The superior performance of the Hellcat over the Zero-sen and the "Oscar" typically gave Naval Aviators the option of simply getting away using the Hellcat's speed and better diving ability to break away and join up with other friendly fighters. If escape was not an option, then the first fundamental principle of defensive tactics was to turn into the attack to present the enemy pilot with a more difficult deflection shot. Thwarting an attack created opportunities for an aggressive response.

Earlier in the war, Wildcat pilots had discovered that the Zero-sen's ailerons stiffened appreciably at high speed, and they developed the technique of pushing over into a steep dive and then turning slightly to the left when attacked from above. When the Zero-sen followed, the Wildcat pilot would then turn hard to the right and pull out of the dive – a maneuver the Zero-sen could not follow. But the US Navy pulled no punches on the reality of being on the defense:

> But when the enemy has numerical superiority over you, the going is really tough. That is when you must employ every trick that you know, all the skill in combat maneuvers you have acquired, all your knowledge of gunnery and all the keen, cool judgement you can muster to get out of the action with a whole skin.

In combat against a determined or lucky foe, all the skill, experience and judgement a pilot had was still sometimes not enough.

CHAPTER 6
COMBAT

After TF 38's successful attacks on Cebu and Negros on September 12–13, 1944 and the apparent weakness of the Japanese response, Adm Halsey decided to mount the first carrier strikes against targets in the area around Manila. In a day of furious combat on September 21, the pilots returned to their carriers and claimed 147 Japanese aircraft shot down and more destroyed on the ground. TF 38 carried out one more day of sweeps over the Visayas before the carriers retired to their anchorages to replenish supplies. In the course of these first carrier strikes on the Philippines, TF 38's carrier squadrons claimed 370 Japanese aircraft shot down in aerial combat and an additional 463 destroyed on the ground. Japanese losses were less than the numbers claimed, but they were still damaging, particularly the continued loss of experienced pilots.

An F6F from VF-8 off USS *Bunker Hill* (CV-17) escorts dive- and torpedo-bombers over Subic Bay on September 21, 1944. Over two days of strikes, TF 38's SB2C Helldivers and TBM Avengers claimed to have destroyed or damaged more than 100 ships of various sizes. (80G-46785, RG80, NARA)

TF 38's support for the planned landings on Leyte, scheduled for October 20, began ten days earlier. Halsey's orders were to first neutralize Japanese air forces at bases north of the Philippines, principally on Formosa, and then pummel Japanese air strength on Luzon in the days leading up to the Leyte invasion. There was an expectation that the Japanese defense of the Philippines would likely involve a fleet action with the IJN's remaining carriers. The Japanese mounted a furious defense of the Philippines, committing hundreds of IJAAF and IJNAF aircraft for determined attacks on TF 38 and the landings on Leyte, and mounting the IJN's last desperate fleet action of the war in the Battle of Leyte Gulf.

The aerial battles over Formosa and the Philippines from October 10–30 were the US Navy's most intensive combats of World War II. During those 20 days Naval Aviators claimed 977 aircraft shot down and 545 destroyed on the ground for the loss of 67 aircraft to Japanese fighters and 128 to anti-aircraft fire. Aerial combat over the Philippines continued during November and December 1944, but at a diminishing rate, with the Fast Carrier Force claiming 272 aircraft shot down during November and 66 in December before ending TF 38's participation in the Philippines campaign in early January 1945. The final months of combat had a different character, for on October 25, 1944 the Japanese initiated the first kamikaze attacks by the IJNAF's hastily organized Special Attack Force, placing new demands on the Hellcat squadrons.

One of the new Hellcat units to enter combat over the Philippines was VF-18, flying off *Intrepid*. On September 21, 1944, Lt Harvey Picken, VF-18's photo officer, was assigned a mission to take post-strike imagery over Clark Field in his F6F-5P, with Lt(jg) Charles Mallory, his assistant photo officer, flying the squadron's second F6F-5P. Coming in from the east, Picken's division saw a flight of G4M "Betty" bombers approaching Clark Field and immediately attacked. Picken, who had previously claimed a Mitsubishi Ki-46 "Dinah" reconnaissance aircraft over Mindanao, shot down a "Betty" and shared a second with his wingman, Lt(jg) George Eckel. The latter also claimed two more "Bettys," while Mallory and his wingman, Lt(jg) Redman Beatley, claimed one each.

As Beatley was finishing his attack on the "Betty," he heard Mallory's warning that Ki-61 "Tony" fighters were taking off from an airfield below. The division soon became involved in a dogfight with several "Tonys," likely from 17th and 19th Sentai who were both active that morning, as the VF-18 Aircraft Action Report recorded:

> BEATLEY had pulled up in a left turn to observe the results of his semi-overhead on his BETTY. As he did so he saw MALLORY finish a run on a TONY which crashed almost beside the burning BETTY. BEATLEY had not as yet realized that other TONYS had taken off from the field. He got the thrill of his life when he looked over his left shoulder and saw 4 TONYs climbing on his tail. MALLORY, pulling out from his pass at the TONY, also observed the 4 TONYs on BEATLEY's tail. MALLORY pulled up in a wingover and made a 70 degree deflection shot at the TONY nearest BEATLEY, getting hits in the Jap's cockpit. The TONY flamed at once. The TONY behind MALLORY's target, meanwhile, got behind MALLORY, who turned inside and made an ahead of the beam pass at this Jap's wingman without result.
>
> MALLORY then observed 6 TONYs climbing for altitude with the obvious intention of gaining the advantage. Calling for his wingman to join up, they commenced climbing at full power using water injection. Starting at 1,200ft, they passed the Japs at 12,000ft, although the latter had a 3,000ft advantage at the beginning. Continuing their climb (ECKEL now joined them), they adopted a gentle weave and turned into the TONYs when they approached. The latter turned away and declined further combat. The climb had continued to 18,000ft.
>
> BEATLEY, on seeing his [Mallory's] predicament, using full power and water injection, started a climbing left turn, shooting at two TONYs, damaging one. PICKEN, who was making a trimetrogon run [aerial photographic survey using

three cameras], heard MALLORY's warning and broke off to lend assistance. He joined the melee, which had largely taken place below the cloud base at 1,000ft. The TONYs he encountered adopted the evasive tactic of a sharp diving turn close to the ground.

PICKEN thought that the Jap pilots seemed to know the ability of their planes to turn inside ours, and used the maneuver time after time trying to get him to spin in. PICKEN succeeded in staying on one TONY's tail long enough to get him burning.

On his way to rendezvous with the rest of his division, Picken saw a Ki-49 "Helen" bomber flying below him and shot it down with his one remaining working gun. This was Picken's third claim for the mission, as he had also shared in the destruction of a "Betty" with Eckel, who shot down two "Bettys" on his own. Mallory claimed a "Betty" and two "Tonys," while Beatley claimed a single "Betty," making it ten victories for the division.

Nichols Field, Nielsen Field and the airfields around the Clark Field area were major targets for the carrier strikes. In addition to inflicting significant damage on airfield installations, the fighters and bombers claimed 173 IJNAF and IJAAF aircraft destroyed on the ground on September 21–22. This photograph of Nichols Field was taken on September 21. (80G-46794, RG80, NARA)

On a second photo mission that afternoon, Picken and Mallory, with two new wingmen, again did battle with a group of "Tonys" from 19th Sentai, claiming four shot down and a fifth shared with a Hellcat from another squadron. Mallory shot down two "Tonys" to add to his morning claims, while Picken added another Tony to his list. Mallory became an ace in two missions on the same day, while Picken added four victories to his previous claim, making him an ace as well. Both men scored in later battles, Mallory ending the war with ten claims and Picken going one better with 11. Beatley and Eckel went on to score two more victories each, just missing ace status.

Nineteen days later, on October 10, TF 38 undertook its first strike on the Ryukyu Islands in support of the pending Leyte invasion. This was followed

Deck crew prepare an F6F-5 from VF-31 on board *Cabot* for a strike against Okinawa on October 10 – note the fighter has been fitted with a replacement cowling from an F6F-3. On that date carrier squadrons claimed 23 Japanese aircraft shot down and 88 destroyed on the ground during sweeps over the Ryukyu Islands. (80G-286513, RG80, NARA)

up 24 hours later by a strike on Aparri, on the northern tip of Luzon. By dawn on October 12, TF 38 was cruising off the east coast of Formosa. The carriers launched a fighter sweep at 0544 hrs with 203 Hellcats to clear the area of Japanese fighters, quickly followed by the first of four strikes against shipping and airfields on Formosa.

The Japanese, forewarned by the attacks on the Ryukyus and Aparri, were ready. 221st Kokutai sent up 43 Zero-sens to intercept the American strike force, with 31 of the new N1K1-J "George" fighters from Sento 401st Hikotai also making their combat debut. The IJAAF dispatched 32 Ki-43s from 20th Sentai and eight Ki-45 "Nick" twin-engined fighters from 3rd Rensei Hikotai, a training unit, and more Ki-43s from a unit staffed by instructor pilots. By chance, 11th Sentai, equipped with Ki-84 "Frank" fighters, was on Formosa on its way to the Philippines, and the unit duly engaged the American carrier aircraft. The Japanese reaction was strong at first, but diminished over the course of the day as more and more fighters went down under the guns of the marauding Hellcats. By dusk TF 38's fighters and bombers had claimed 224 Japanese aircraft shot down.

Leading one of four divisions launched by VF-8 from *Bunker Hill* that morning was Lt Ernest Beauchamp. He would experience a remarkable mission, claiming three Japanese aircraft destroyed, one probably destroyed and three damaged for his first claims in combat. Beauchamp subsequently recalled:

Someone tally-hoed bogies at 10 o'clock. We turned into them and I took a shot at one that split-S'ed. The next one I saw dived for the ground and I dived after it. I was able to get off a short burst, but another F6F interfered before it burned and I believe the pilot of that one claimed the plane. However, I did damage to it.

We then effected a rendezvous and proceeded towards Matsuyama. As we approached Taien at about 8,000ft, an *Intrepid* pilot reported planes taking off from the airfield. Bogies were being tally-hoed also, and I spotted about eight twin-engined planes to port – "Nicks," I believe. I signaled left and turned into a three-plane section, shooting one down in flames from a 60-degree deflection run. I then spotted a plane flying low over the field and dived on him. I smoked it, but my excessive speed caused me to over-shoot and another F6F shot it down after several runs.

I then began to climb, and when at 4,500ft, "Zekes" were reported coming down out of the clouds. I pushed everything forward and engaged my first "Oscar" at about 6,000ft. There was a two-plane section, one of them shooting at an F6F. I took a snap shot, and the "Oscar" smoked and dived away. Someone was shooting at the other one as it went out of my range of vision.

There seemed to be a lull then of two or three minutes, during which time I climbed for altitude; I joined a lone F6F. The sequence of events are hazy from here on in as the fighting began in earnest. The lull was broken suddenly by another group of "Oscars" coming down from the upper layer of clouds. I made a run on one, and he smoked first and then broke into flames as I overshot him. This put me on the outside of things and very much alone, except for a "Zeke" which made a strong effort to eliminate me. There was nothing to do except take evasive action and work back to the center of things. I did this successfully and some F6Fs took care of the situation.

Then there was a period of scissoring and tight turning, 50-50 between the Japs and me. How many bursts I shot and at how many planes I couldn't be sure, but

44

I believe about four. One of these smoked and split-S'ed. There is a question in my mind whether he could have made the pull-out in time, but due to low clouds I did not see the result.

I climbed back to 8,000ft and attempted to stay in a populated area. I found myself on the inside of an "Oscar" with only two of my guns working. I saw hits on his wing, but I didn't think very serious damage had been done when the dumb Jap bailed out. About this time I heard a call for help and at the same time saw an "Oscar" low on the ground. Thinking this might be the one causing the trouble, I made a run on him, but only one gun fired and then stopped altogether before I could see any results. I broke off then and returned to the area of the epic conflict, but things appeared to be under control. Pilots were reporting that they were out of ammunition and low on gas. We rendezvoused and returned to the carrier.

The next day, Beauchamp claimed a "Dinah" for his final victory, bringing his total to four destroyed. His wingman, Lt(jg) Peter Van Der Linden, claimed three "Oscars" shot down on October 12 to add to a "Tony" he had claimed over Manila on September 21. He too would claim one more victory to "make ace." In total, VF-8 was credited with 50 Japanese aircraft shot down on October 12, with five more probably shot down and 19 damaged.

VF-19 sent four divisions on the first fighter sweep, where they ran into 30 to 40 Japanese fighters. The encounter degenerated into a free for all, with the F6Fs in the center of the melee. The VF-19 pilots thought that there were six or seven Ki-44 "Tojos" and possibly

ABOVE
An F6F-3 of VF-19 is cleared for take-off from the USS *Lexington* (CV-16) on October 12 – the first day of strikes against Japanese air strength on Formosa. For TF 38's pilots this would be a day of intense aerial combat, with fighter and bomber crews claiming 224 Japanese aircraft shot down in total. (80G-285037, RG80, NARA)

LEFT
VF-19 Hellcats return to the *Lexington* after a strike mission on Formosa on October 12. The squadron claimed 33 Japanese aircraft shot down during the day's combats. The F6F in the foreground already sports two Japanese flags below the cockpit. (80G-285045, RG80, NARA)

Airmen prepare VT-8 TBM Avengers and VF-8 F6F-3 Hellcats on board *Bunker Hill* for the second day of strikes against Formosa on October 13. There were far fewer air combats that day, with claims for only 37 Japanese aircraft shot down. (80G-298609, RG80, NARA)

some "Tonys" in the mix of "Zekes" that came down on them. These were more likely to have been the N1K1-J "George" fighters of Sento 401st Hikotai, as IJAAF and IJNAF fighters rarely flew in mixed formations.

Leading one of VF-19's divisions, Lt Joseph Paskoski would claim one of these "Tonys" destroyed and another damaged, along with three other Japanese fighters, in a mission that ended in a successful water landing. He noted in his Aircraft Action Report:

After reaching the area south of Kagi on Formosa, our fighters led by Lt Cdr COOK, flew directly under a large number of "Zekes" who had about 4,000ft altitude advantage over us. We were at 16,000ft (approximately). One "Zeke" started a run, rolling over slowly, but pulled out as he saw me pull up slightly toward him. My effort, however, would have been futile for we were cruising at 130 knots and speed was quickly lost from the steep pull up. (Note: I recommend that all formations in vicinity of enemy aircraft, especially if enemy has altitude advantage, fly at a speed which will enable worthwhile countering maneuvers). This "Zeke" did not dive again – others remained intact also. I called Lt Cdr COOK, reporting the superior number above, but was unable to alter our precarious position (more speed would have been advantageous). We continued north and I soon lost sight of the "Zekes" above. They disappeared in the sun.

Minutes later I tally-hoed from three to six "Zekes" below us on the way up. They kept coming without attack, so I led my division down on them. I set one afire in an overhead run slightly astern in about a 70° degree dive. Also observed my wingman set one on fire – both plummeted earthward. This apparently brought the high-flying "Zekes" down upon my four planes. In pulling out of my first run I hit another "Zeke" square from behind – 0° deflection. He fell afire.

By this time the planes were fighting everywhere. The next few minutes I was busy eluding "Zekes" and chasing them off other F6Fs' tails. Parachutes began to appear

– at one time I counted four. Then suddenly the "Zekes" disappeared, apparently all shot down. Spotting two "Nates" at about 4,000ft, I dove on one and hit him from behind and above in about a 30° degree dive. He fell into the water after a long shallow glide aflame. The other, with his superior turning ability, kept me off his tail. I climbed into the sun, got above him and came down in a run (high-side), but he easily turned out of my sights. Tried same again – this time he did a split-S at 2,000ft. I had to recover without following his maneuver. He escaped and I rejoined the group at 9,000–11,000ft.

We proceeded north once again. Someone tallyhoed a "Tony" at 3 o'clock below. I spotted him and made a high-side run, getting sucked astern as he turned away. I set him smoking badly with a no deflection shot. With only two guns working, I had considerable trouble finishing him. Also, the necessity of re-charging after each burst made it difficult to stay on him. I pulled away so my wingman could finish the job, but an alert Rebel plane with six guns slipped in to do the trick. This I'm sure peeved my wingman.

We started climbing to rejoin, and were attacked by a single "Tony." He came from behind and pulled out foolishly directly in front, enabling me to jump on his tail immediately. Adding water injection, he was soon in range. Spurting and recharging alternately, I set him smoking fiercely. He then flew in a straight line 10–20ft from the ground, rocking his wings with canopy open. A few more bursts and he still remained in the air. I pulled off to allow my wingman to finish him but he couldn't shoot because his gunsight wasn't working (I learned later). Once again I took over and succeeded in starting a good fire. He crashed into the maze of rice paddies below.

We reformed and opened out in defensive formation, before proceeding homeward alone. My tail being hit, I was directed to make a water landing – tail hook would not extend. A few minutes later I was recovered by a destroyer, which incidentally did a fine piece of rescue work.

Paskoski had flown the entire combat mission with a depth charge under his wing that he had been unable to jettison when enemy fighters were engaged. Paskoski's wingman, Lt Bernard Garbow, shot down two "Zekes" and a "Nate" for his only claims of the war. On this one mission VF-19 claimed 33 fighters shot down, four more as probables and a further 12 damaged for the loss of Lt Cdr Franklin E. Cook and Lt Donald K. Tripp, both of whom were shot down by either Japanese fighters or anti-aircraft fire while strafing Taichu airfield.

Despite having suffered heavy losses over Formosa, the IJNAF still had a cadre of experienced pilots who were both capable and dangerous. This was proved at 1835 hrs on October 13 when a torpedo dropped by a B6N2 "Jill" hit the heavy cruiser USS *Canberra* (CA-70) whilst it was sailing off Formosa, damaging the ship so badly that

Ens Edward Phillips of VF-20, embarked in USS *Enterprise* (CV-6), climbs out of his Hellcat after flying a mission to Formosa on October 13. Forty-eight hours prior to this photograph being taken, Phillips had claimed four "Zekes" shot down in one mission. He would make one further claim on October 18 to become an ace. (80G-298134, RG80, NARA)

Lt Charlie Stimpson finished the war as VF-11's ranking ace with 16 victories. He was one of a handful of Naval Aviators who claimed five or more kills in both the F4F and F6F. "Skull" Stimpson became one of the deadliest fighter pilots in the US Navy, usually scoring in multiples, including five victories off the coast of Formosa on October 14. He ended the conflict as the US Navy's seventh ranking fighter ace, tied with Lt Ira Kepford of VF-17 and Lt(jg) Douglas Baker of VF-20. (US Navy)

it had to be taken under tow by the heavy cruiser USS *Wichita* (CA-45). During its slow withdrawal from the area the cruiser was covered by CAPs from TF 38's Hellcats.

During October 14 the IJNAF again launched several attacks on TF 38 warships cruising 120 miles off the coast of Formosa. In the early afternoon, two divisions from VF-11 were flying a regular CAP over their Task Group (TG) 38.1 when they received a vector to a large contact approaching the vessels. When Lt Nelson Dayhoff, leading the two divisions, lost his radio and Lt Jimmie Savage, leading the second division, had his compass fail, Lt Charlie Stimpson, leading the second section in Dayhoff's division, took over the lead. Savage "tally-hoed" the bandits, which Stimpson estimated were eight to 12 D4Y "Judy" dive-bombers, with an escort of 15–20 Zero-sens. The CAP was then flying at 17,000ft, above the bombers and level with the fighters. Stimpson ordered his fighters to attack, as he recorded in his Aircraft Action Report:

As my second section and Lt Savage's division were below and to my left, it gave them a better position to attack the bombers. I figured that if my section could engage and occupy the Zeros immediately above, their chance to get the combers [dive-bombers] would be improved. As it so happened this was the way it worked, for they destroyed five to seven of the bombers on the first pass before the top cover hit them.

The element of surprise was with us for they made no move to show they had seen us. I picked as my first target three "Hamps" flying in a tight V formation just above the bombers. I closed fast from slightly below and astern and held my fire until I was within boresight range. They all carried two large external gas tanks below their wings, and the attack was such a surprise that I flamed all three before they dropped any and made any attempt to break. In order not to over-run the third, after I had flamed the first, I had to cut my throttle completely and still had to pull up to miss him as he burst into flames.

As I pulled up I saw a "Zeke" below me diving on my second division. I rolled over in an overhead pass and he exploded after a short burst. On my pull out there was a "Zeke" slightly above, but just as I pulled into firing range and opened up he split S'd out and I was unable to see if I damaged him. I didn't follow, as I wanted to use my excess speed to regain my lost altitude. For a minute I feared I was alone, as the overhead pass had carried me away from the fight, but as I looked back I saw my wingman, Ens [Fred] Blair, directly on my tail. I had seen him flame one Zero on our first pass, and later in the fight saw him take two more off my tail.

I saw a fight still going on, and it looked as though a couple of F6Fs were badly outnumbered. We dove back in, and the first target I saw was a "Tony" dead ahead on the tail of one of our planes. I closed on him in a steep high-side and fired two long bursts into him. He was so intent on his target he did not see me, and I hit him badly. His engine threw out black smoke and I last saw him as he was going straight down. Lt Savage, on whose tail this "Tony" was, saw him fall off, smoking badly. Things were pretty warm at this time and I was unable to watch him crash, and thus do not claim him, but I feel sure he never pulled out from that dive.

By this time we were under pretty constant attack. Ens Blair, who had gone after another Zero on another F6F's tail, and got him, came at me and we pulled our defensive scissor. As we crossed the second time, I got a good shot at another "Tony" on Ens Blair's tail. I saw my bullets hitting him in the cowling, engine and wing roots, and he also smoked and fell off. I feel sure it was self-sealing tanks which kept those two from burning. I was carried a little wide by firing at this "Tony," and as I scissored back I saw a "Zeke" firing at Blair. As I crossed I opened fire and must have hit his wing gas tank, for it exploded and blew off his port wing.

Blair had been hit and I saw his belly tank on fire. I told him to drop it and dive for the deck. I crossed over him as he headed down, but only one "Zeke" attempted to follow, and he scared off when I fired my remaining ammunition in front of him. Blair was losing altitude and the flames seem to spread to the lower part of his engine. I saw he couldn't make it, and he made a water landing a few seconds later. The sea was very rough and he hit very hard. I circled him, but could see no one get out, and as soon as the plane sank there was no way of keeping track of the spot. It is my belief that he got out, however, as he obviously made a controlled landing. I returned to the ship and gave as close a position report on him as possible, but as yet have had no word of his rescue.

Upon my return I found that of the seven who followed me into the attack three were missing, including Ens Blair. Lt Dayhoff's wingman informed us that Lt Dayhoff destroyed one "Judy" for sure and then was hit by a Zero attacking from above. He must have been killed instantly for he rolled over and spun straight on down. Lt(jg) [Sam] Goldberg was never seen after the fight began, but his wingman returned to the carrier badly hit by shrapnel in the arm and head, making an excellent no wheels/no flaps landing.

Whether I was correct in attacking or whether I should have awaited help is not for me to decide, but according to our score we destroyed five for every man we lost. Also, we broke up the attack, which I feel sure they intended to make.

The seven Naval Aviators together claimed 13 Japanese aircraft shot down and four more as probables for the loss of three pilots. Stimpson claimed three "Hamps" and two "Zekes" destroyed, and the two "Tonys" he encountered as probables – his first claims since he became an ace fighting over Guadalcanal

Parked in front of eight SB2Cs and five TBMs, three HVAR-armed F6F-5s from VF-20 Hellcats await their pilots on the flightdeck of *Enterprise* prior to flying a mission against airfields in the Manila area on October 15. Clearly the carrier has been alerted to the threat of enemy aircraft in the area as virtually all the personnel visible in this photograph (including at least one of the pilots) are wearing steel helmets. (80G-284609, RG80, NARA)

in 1943. For his initiative and courage in taking this action that likely saved his Task Group from attack, Stimpson was awarded the Navy Cross.

Over the next several days the Hellcat pilots of TF 38 were heavily engaged in aerial combat as the IJNAF launched repeated attacks on the Task Force in the forlorn hope of destroying American carriers before the looming invasion of the Philippines could begin. At the same time, TF 38 struck Japanese air strength on Luzon and the Visayas prior to the scheduled landings on Leyte.

During October 15, TG 38.1 proceeded to a refueling rendezvous point 120 miles off the east coast of Luzon, coming under attack throughout the day. The Japanese launched 11 raids against the Task Group in short succession, comprising three large attacks of ten to 20 aircraft and smaller attacks in groups of two to ten aircraft. TG 38.1's CAP fighters claimed 52 Japanese aircraft destroyed during continuous patrols.

VF-14's pilots were scrambled repeatedly from *Wasp* for CAP missions. Lt William Knight, who had scored earlier in the combats over the Visayas, led one of the divisions, with Lt(jg) R. A. Taylor as his wingman, and Lt(jg) J. Sisk leading his second section with Ens L. A. Dewing as his No. 2. A third section, led by Lt F. E. Standring, with Lt(jg) C. M. Houston as his wingman, made up the CAP. Their experiences that day, recorded in the squadron's Aircraft Action Report, were similar to other Hellcat pilots flying CAP over TF 38's formations on October 15:

Lt. Knight's division, together with Lt. Standring and his wingman, were vectored 260 degrees Buster, angels 15 [15,000ft], for about 60 miles but were unable to contact any bogies. They started to orbit and lost some altitude when Lt. Knight tally-hoed two "Zekes" 400 to 500 yards from Lt. Standring and on the latter's tail, with six to eight more coming down on his own division out of the clouds above. He called a warning to Lt. Standring and then turned his division into the attacking planes, but was unable to bear on them. Finally he got a shot at one from 200 to 300 yards away at between 1 and 2 o'clock – this plane started smoking and it went into a shallow dive and the pilot bailed out.

There was another "Zeke" near the one which Lt. Knight had just shot down, but he turned 240 degrees and started running off in a long glide. He had already nearly two miles distance between himself and Lt. Knight, but the latter, using full power, gave chase and closed to about 400 yards in three minutes. As the "Zeke" was heading for a cloud, Lt. Knight fired a burst and believed he got some hits, as the "Zeke" burned and then went into the cloud at about 2000ft. Lt. Knight followed him in, still closing, and when they came out, he was only about 300 yards behind. He gave the Jap three short bursts, which started his plane smoking and the pilot rolled it to starboard and bailed out at about 1,000ft. Lt(jg) Taylor also got a good full deflection burst into the plane before it crashed in the water. Lt. Knight's flight then rendezvoused and headed back to the carrier.

While Lt. Knight was shooting down his first plane, Lt(jg) Taylor also splashed one of the "Zekes" which had made a high-side attack on the division, and believed he damaged a second. During the melee, Lt(jg) Taylor was using full throttle and 2,700rpm.

Lt(jg) J. Sisk and his wingman chased a "Zeke" in a shallow full-speed dive for 15 miles and were only able to close about a mile on him during this time. Prior to this, Lt(jg) Sisk had shot down a "Zeke" in a modified high-side attack, and

Ens. Dewing, his wingman, shot down two, one from directly astern, one in a head-on run, and probably destroyed a third with a full deflection burst which started the Jap smoking badly, but he was not seen to crash.

Lt. Standring and Lt(jg) Houston, after they heard Lt. Knight's warning of the two "Zekes" diving on their tails, looked up and saw them, as well as the "Zekes" attacking Lt. Knight's division, which was about 1,000ft above them. Lt. Standring and Lt(jg) Houston nosed over into a shallow port turn and gained speed to 300 knots IAS [indicated air speed] waiting for the "Zekes" to close and start firing. As soon as they did, Lt. Standring pulled back on his stick, causing the "Zekes" to overrun him, but they stayed on Lt(jg) Houston's tail. This enabled Lt. Standring to whip back onto the tail of the nearest one. When Lt. Standring started firing, the Jap made a turn to starboard, rolled over on his back, went on down nose first and crashed.

Seeing Lt. Knight's division engaged in a melee, Lt. Standring joined in, and spotted an F6F with a "Zeke" on its tail. He made a climbing beam run, firing into the Jap and knocking pieces out of his fuselage and wing. His engine belched black smoke and he pulled up over Lt. Standring and bailed out.

At one time during the melee, Lt. Standring saw four parachutes in the air, all of which he believes were Japs. Planes seemed to be falling and exploding all around. After two minutes there were no Jap planes left in that area, and upon returning to base the FDO [Flight Deck Officer] told all fighters that this particular bogie completely disappeared, indicating that they had knocked down most of them. It would appear that these six planes had splashed ten of the 12 they encountered.

The VF-14 pilots found that the Zero-sens they ran into on this mission were flown very aggressively. The Aircraft Action Report noted that "they appeared to attempt to maintain a semblance of formation. Their attacks were mostly overhead, high-side and head-on, while their evasive maneuvers consisted

0900 hrs, OCTOBER 17, 1944

MANILA BAY

1 Lt Bruce A. McGraw is leading a division of four F6Fs from VF-13 at 22,000ft over the Manila Bay area when he sees several formations of enemy aircraft climbing below him.

2 McGraw maneuvers his division (comprising Ens Nicholas J. Smith, Lt(jg) Robert F. Brooks and Ens Robert V. Hungerford) into a position up-sun before diving down on a formation of four IJAAF Ki-61 "Tonys" flying at 15,000ft, coming in from astern.

3 The "Tonys" turn to the left as the F6Fs close and open fire, at which point the Japanese formation attempts to scatter. Three of the "Tonys" go down in flames, and the pilot of the fourth fighter bails out of his smoking Ki-61.

4 McGraw takes his division back up to 22,000ft, where he spots another formation of three "Tonys" below him and dives down on them.

5 Spotting the rapidly descending Hellcats, the "Tony" pilots dive into a nearby cloud bank at 15,000ft in an attempt to lose their pursuers.

6 McGraw leads his division around the cloud bank and jumps the "Tonys" as they emerge from the other side. All three Ki-61s are swiftly shot down.

Lt Edward Turner joined the US Navy in January 1941 and had completed the bulk of his flight training before the attack on Pearl Harbor. Flying with VF-14 off *Wasp*, Turner claimed four "Zekes" and an "Oscar" destroyed during a strike against the airfield at Mabalacat, near Clark Field, on October 18. (80G-349847, RG80, NARA)

of the usual aerobatics – slight climbing turns, flipper turns, rolls, loops, wing-overs, split-Ss, jinking, etc., and jumping in and out of clouds. Speeds varied up to 330 knots, indicated, at 13,000ft with full power settings. Their gunnery was far inferior to ours. Our planes maintained formation, stuck together, and protected each other."

VF-14 also participated in the strikes on the airfields around the Manila area on Luzon. On October 18, the unit sent three divisions of mixed F6F-3 and F6F-5 Hellcats on a sweep over the airfields in central Luzon around Clark Field, flying with two divisions from VF-11. The Hellcats ran into a mixed formation of very aggressive Japanese fighters they identified as "Zekes" and "Oscars." As the Aircraft Action Report recorded, the Japanese aircraft "could be caught in level flight, and in most cases, our planes could turn into them and get on an opposite course. In a few instances the ZEKES and OSCARS outclimbed and outmaneuvered our F6F-3s and -5s, but in general they made over-head passes and head-on runs, then went into evasive dives and the usual split-S, rolls, etc., pulling out radically just off the ground. Their camouflage was very effective, blending with the landscape, and the pilots utilized their familiarity with the terrain to fly up valleys and ravines."

Lt Edward Turner was leading VF-14's third division that morning. He had trained as a Naval Aviator during 1941 and had served as an instructor before joining VF-14 in September 1943. Prior to the day's mission, he had claimed a "Zeke" during the Marianas Turkey Shoot and an "Irving" on October 15 during VF-14's defense of TG 38.1. Over Mabalacat, Turner would claim four "Zekes" and an "Oscar" shot down, becoming an "ace in a day" in his final combat of the war.

The VF-14 and VF-11 divisions went down to strafe an airfield near Clark Field, setting eight twin-engined aircraft on fire. After his strafing run, Turner led his division back up to rejoin Lt K. W. Garwood, leading the VF-14 divisions flying high cover at 8,000ft. The unit's Aircraft Action Report stated:

Lt(jg) W. E. Schmidt, leader of Lt. Turner's second section, was slightly behind and closing, when he was jumped by an "Oscar" out of the clouds, which hit him just behind and in the cockpit. Lt(jg) Schmidt's plane started to disintegrate and went into a spin and crashed. The "Oscar" split S'ed down towards the field, and Lt. Turner split-S'ed out after him and followed him down, firing until he was forced to pull out at 500ft. The "Tony" [sic] kept right on going and crashed. Lt. Turner then climbed back up and again joined with Lt. Garwood's division at 8,000ft.

The flight went on to Clark Field, encountering some heavy AA fire. Lt. Turner spotted a "Zeke" going for a landing on the fields, and made a diving attack on it. The "Zeke" crashed and burned. Lt(jg) Haas, who was with Turner, also got some hits on this plane. Again climbing back up to join Lt. Garwood's division, Lt. Turner spotted a "Zeke" some distance behind at 10,000ft. He called Lt. Garwood and told him he was going back after him and turned to do so. As he and Lt(jg) Haas commenced to close on the "Zeke," six more of them came out of a cloud behind the approaching plane. Lt. Turner and Lt(jg) Haas scored hits on the initial "Zeke," which nosed over after it had fired at them. They followed it down and shot it down. Lt. Turner got his next plane – another "Zeke" – low over the trees with only two guns working. The pilot bailed out at 400ft.

Lt. Turner then climbed back up and joined up on Lt(jg) Guenzi while the latter shot down a "Zeke," which had made an over-head pass at him. Lt. Turner and Lt(jg) Guenzi climbed back to 6,000ft and another Zeke came towards them, and pulled up into Turner, then whipped onto Turner's tail as the latter made a climbing turn. However, the "Zeke" then fell off and pulled his nose up while Lt. Turner came over on top of him. The "Zeke" dove for the ground and his tail came off as he tried to pull out. Lt. Turner blacked out as he pulled out, and recovered to find a "Zeke" on his tail which was firing at him, hitting his F6F around its port fuselage, fin and port wing. Lt. J. B. Mongogna came along and shot this plane off Lt. Turner's tail. Lt. Turner got in a shot at another "Zeke" which smoked, but was knocked down by four other F6Fs.

The Aircraft Action Report for the mission included the observation that many of the aircraft encountered seemed to have better armor and fuel-tank protection than the Japanese fighters the Hellcat pilots had previously fought. It is quite possible that among the aircraft the Naval Aviators thought were "Zekes" and "Oscars" were the new N1K1-J Shiden (codenamed "George") fighters of 341st Kokutai or Sento 701st Hikotai, which had recently arrived in the Philippines.

Lt Turner included comments on tactics employed against the Japanese fighters. He found that "the most successful tactics against overhead attacks are to climb up into them, scissoring, and the instant the enemy plane passes in his dive, split-S out and jump on his tail. This maneuver should not be attempted except by a four-plane division, as it appears to be the Jap practice to send one plane down to make a pass, and others wait above to jump our planes if they get strung out or separated. The second section following down should weave to protect the first, and keep a sharp lookout overhead and behind. The Jap planes are able to pull out of their dives much lower and more sharply than the F6Fs. They could split-S at 1,500ft and come out right over the tree-tops. The counter maneuver recommended by Lt. Turner when they go into this maneuver at such low altitudes is to do a wing-over so as to be in a position to pull out safely."

The landing of US Army Rangers on a small island off Leyte on October 17 alerted the Japanese to the impending invasion and led the IGH command to issue orders for *Sho No. 1* in defense of the Philippines. The IJN's much-diminished carrier force in Japan planned to sail toward Luzon to lure Adm Halsey's TF 38 away, thus allowing the still formidable Japanese battleship force to attack the American invasion fleet off Leyte. IJAAF aircraft were rushed to the Philippines, as were land-based types of the IJNAF.

On a sweep over Manila on October 17 Lt Bruce McGraw's division claimed eight aircraft shot down. Here, McGraw (left) describes to VF-13's Executive Officer and Intelligence Officer how he shot down a "Tony" and shared a second with his wingman, Ens Nicholas Smith. (80G-290743, RG80, NARA)

The Battle of Leyte Gulf took place on October 24–25. In the days immediately prior to the battle, TF 38 aircraft carried out strikes on southern Luzon and the Visayas in support of the Leyte landings and long-range patrols in search of the approaching Japanese fleets. The climactic battle of the aerial campaign over the Philippines took place on October 24, when TF 38's carrier pilots and the Hellcat and FM-2 Wildcat pilots from the escort carriers in the Seventh Fleet's TG 77.4 claimed 270 enemy aircraft shot down. Only the claims for Japanese aircraft during the Marianas Turkey Shoot exceeded this total.

VF-19 had sent off several divisions on the early morning search missions, and after these had returned, it scrambled many fighters to intercept incoming Japanese raids shortly after 0700 hrs. Flying on the latter missions were senior lieutenants Elvin Lindsay and William Masoner, with several more junior pilots making up their divisions. Masoner had served ashore with VF-11 at Guadalcanal in 1943, where he had claimed two "Zekes," while Lindsay and the others were new to combat, having made their first claims in the recent aerial battles over Formosa and Manila. Their experiences on this day would once again show the importance of opportunity in aerial combat, and the excellence of their training and their aircraft.

Shortly after dawn, VF-19 sent out four divisions of four Hellcats and one division of three as escorts to 18 SB2Cs of VB-19, with four fighters acting as a radio relay team back to TG 38.3. Each team of Hellcats and Helldivers

covered a compass bearing sector. Lt Lindsay was leading his division in an attack on some small ships near Lingayen Gulf when they heard the bombers call out bogies. VF-19's Aircraft Action Report noted:

> Giving full throttle, they soon encountered a number of "Tojos" in the neighborhood of Clark Field and saw the bombers ducking into the clouds. Lt. LINDSAY and his wingman, Ens. MARTIN, were attacked by ten "Tojos," which were soon put on the defensive by our two planes which immediately turned into the attack. The "Tojos" broke up into a disorganized group, their runs were poorly timed and lacked coordination and they finally went into a tail chase. They attacked singly or in loose pairs, and as our two stayed together and protected each other's tails, they were able to handle the situation comfortably, although Ens. MARTIN, because of damage to his plane, was forced to make a water landing alongside a destroyer on his return to the task group.
>
> Lt. LINDSAY caught one "Tojo" from 7 o'clock level, saw tracers enter the fuselage, flames and heavy smoke break out and the fighter then plunge straight down. He then caught another in the same way, but it did not flame and although apparently going in, was not observed to crash. Another was centered in a suicide head-on run, from which Lt. LINDSAY had to pull up to avoid crashing, and these two are classed as probables. He then went down to 3,000ft, zooming under a "Val" to avoid the rear gunner, who was shooting, and got in a severe burst centering the cockpit. This plane was seen to crash by Ens. MARTIN.
>
> Ens. MARTIN himself first smoked two "Tojos" with deflection shots and they dove into the clouds but results could not be observed, then he caught one that was making a run on Lt. LINDSAY. Making a quick turn and getting on his tail, a burst brought pieces from his wing. The "Tojo" then split S'ed and his wing tore off. Another came head on but turned away as MARTIN began to fire. Turning with him, MARTIN gave a little extra lead and let him run into his bullets. The "Tojo" burst into flames and dove straight down. MARTIN came down on a "Val" in a high-side run, which he flattened out to get on his tail and saw the "Val" crash.

Cdr Hugh Winters (left), the commander of CAG-19, presents an award to Lt Elvin Lindsay during a ceremony held on the flightdeck of *Lexington* in November 1944. Lindsay, who earned the Navy Cross, two Silver Stars and a Distinguished Flying Cross during his tour with VF-19, had assumed command of the unit on November 5. He was the third, and last, CO of VF-19 during its deployment, the squadron having lost three commanding officers in less than two months over the Philippines. Aged just 24 when put in charge of VF-19, Lindsay was almost certainly the youngest US Navy squadron commander of World War II. (80G-287815, RG80, NARA)

In the space of just a few minutes Lindsay had shot down a "Tojo" and a "Val" and claimed two more as probables, while Martin had shot down two "Tojos" and a "Val," and damaged two more "Tojos." The two other pilots in Lindsay's division, Lt E. F. Schoch and Ens A. L. Price, claimed three more "Tojos" shot down.

Lt William Masoner's division, sent on a search to the north of Lt Lindsay's sector, had even more success. Masoner and his three pilots ran into several formations of unescorted Japanese bombers and claimed 13 shot down. Masoner gave the following account of the one-sided clash in the squadron Aircraft Action Report:

We took off at 0610. My division escorting four SB2Cs on a 300-mile search from 275° to 285°. We entered a front spreading from about 50 miles from the ship to about 20 miles inland. We flew instruments for 25 minutes, and on emerging from the front the bombers were out of sight. We finally spotted them circling at 8,000ft over the eastern shore of Lingayen Gulf (Luzon). As we came up to join them they spotted a group of "Bettys" and I saw them shoot down two. I saw four or five "Bettys" scattering in all directions. I picked one and went down on it with my division. I opened with a quartering shot and rode up on his tail. I observed his 20mm gun firing from his turret. My incendiaries hit his fuselage and right wing root. He burst into flames and hit the water.

I pulled up from this attack and saw eight "Dinahs" about 100ft over me. They turned and spread slightly. I came up from below the right hand plane and put a long burst into his starboard engine. It started to burn – the flames spread and it fell in a mass of flames. During this time I saw four or five flamers and smokers crash on the shore. By this time no more planes were available, so we rendezvoused and continued on our search.

After about 50 miles one of the [SB2C] bombers tallyhoed two "Nells." We dove down after them and chased them for five or six miles. I dropped my bomb and then caught up with them. I made a run from above and astern and his right wing burned, exploded and fell off. He dove into the water and burned. I started to make a run on the other "Nell" but he was burning already and crashed. My wingman (Copeland) got him. These "Nells" had the new ball turret on their backs, and one of these hit my section leader's engine. He was able to proceed, however.

We then joined the bombers – flew our cross leg and started home.

As we approached the shore of Luzon we spotted five "Nells" at about 500 ft. My wingman and I dived down on them and he burned one, which crashed. His guns then stopped and he pulled up with Bennett, (whose engine was damaged). I made a high quartering run on one "Nell" and observed hits. I did a wing over and came up under his tail to avoid his ball turret, which was firing. I hit him in the fuselage at very close range. He exploded and pieces flew all over. He nosed straight down and hit the water – there was no fire. I came from behind and above the next "Nell" and, hit in the wing root, he exploded, throwing large pieces by me as I pulled up. He burned and crashed.

This left two "Nells" out of the original five. I made two passes on one of them, and on the second rode his tail until he burst into flames. We were very low, and he hit [the ground] immediately. By this time Davis (my No. 4 man) had come down from escorting the bombers and we chased the last "Nell" over the land. We each had one gun firing, and though we both got good hits, it wouldn't burn. My guns had stopped entirely by this time, so we withdrew.

In this action Masoner claimed six bombers shot down and a probable, while his wingman Lt(jg) W. E. Copeland claimed three. His second section leader Lt E. E. Bennett claimed two, as did Bennett's wingman, Lt(jg) W. E. Davis. Later that morning, TG 38.3 sent out search teams of four Hellcats and four Helldivers to locate elements of the IJN fleet. F6Fs also undertook a fighter sweep over the airfields around Manila. A large force of Japanese aircraft approached the Task Group, but they were beaten off. TG 38.3 then sent off a strike force to attack a large enemy surface force moving toward the

San Bernadino Straits. Shortly after noon, another large group of Japanese aircraft showed up on radar approaching the Task Group, followed by a second group a short while later.

Following the detection of these formations, TG 38.3 quickly launched more Hellcats. Amongst the aircraft sent aloft were six fighters from VF-19 led by Lt Lindsay. Running into Zero-sens, Lindsay quickly flamed two "Zekes," as did the other division leader, Lt H. J. Rossi. Ens Paul O'Mara, flying wing on Rossi's section leader, also got two "Zekes" in quick succession. He detailed the combat in his Aircraft Action Report:

> Engaged five to seven "Zekes" at approximately 4,000ft altitude off the port quarter of the Task Group at a distance of approximately 15 miles (after being vectored out). First saw three "Zekes" flying in column. Approaching from 5 o'clock, I picked the second one. Before I could get into range, he split S'd, setting me up for a good overhead, which I pressed home – but had forgotten to put on my master arming switch.
>
> "Zeke" made a run on me from 7 o'clock high, but broke off when I started to turn into him. He pulled up into a high wingover, which gave me a short burst from 4 o'clock and below. I gave him one burst, which hit him in the right wing root and wing tanks – he caught fire and pulled up into a small cloud. I did not follow. Ens McPherson saw him splash ("Zeke" had two small wing tanks similar to SB2C).
>
> I then saw a "Zeke" make a run on two F6Fs from 6 o'clock level – pulled into him from 3 o'clock and gave him a short burst, and he broke away to the left and pulled up in a high wing over. I followed and gave him another short burst from 6 o'clock below, which caught him in the belly tank and he began to stream gas. He then split S'd, which I followed. He pulled up and I hit him with a long burst from 6 o'clock below to 6 o'clock above – he caught fire and spun. The "Zeke" broke in half behind the cockpit before it hit the water.

Shortly before dusk TF 38's search aircraft located the IJN carrier force, but it was too late in the day to get off a strike. The following morning (October 25), TGs 38.2 and 38.3 sent out five strikes against the Japanese carriers, located some 135 miles away. CAG-15 had taken off from *Essex* at dawn and was waiting for a contact report. When it came, the Carrier Air Group was only 50 miles away from the Japanese force. Cdr David McCampbell led 14 Hellcats from VF-15. While he remained above as high cover and target coordinator, ten Hellcats armed with 500lb bombs went down to bomb and strafe the enemy ships ahead of the dive- and torpedo-bombers. One of the IJN carriers had managed to launch around 20 Zero-sens, which were attacked by Lt John Strane's division. The Hellcat pilots involved claimed eight shot down and three more as probables. Strane, however, was shot down in flames, although he managed to bail out. According to VF-15's Aircraft Action Report:

> After recovery from bombing and strafing the carriers, Lt. Strane noticed five or six "Zekes" at 10 o'clock up at 9,000ft. The VBs [SB2Cs] were retiring below, so Strane's team followed and covered, climbing, but did not turn towards the bogies until they started a run.

Cdr David McCampbell, leading CAG-15 embarked in *Essex*, was the standout US Navy ace of the fighting over the Philippines. Between September 12 and November 14, 1944 he claimed 23.5 victories, nine of them on October 24. (80G-K-2178, RG80, NARA)

Naval Aviators gather around the tail of a well-weathered F6F-3 from VF-18 on board *Intrepid* after completing strikes on the airfields around Clark Field on October 29. The unit claimed 35 Japanese aircraft shot down that day, with the squadron's ranking ace, Lt Cecil Harris, leading the way with three "Tojos" and a "Zeke" destroyed. (80G-291044, RG80, NARA)

On the first contact he flamed a "Zeke" as it was pulling off from his attack, getting in full deflection bursts from 3 o'clock down, and saw this plane crash in the water, along with two other splashes. Next thing he noticed was his wingman start a diving turn to the left, and as he rolled over he saw two "Zekes" firing at the wingman. He continued in his dive and was in an excellent position astern and above both, and flamed them both – one from 5 o'clock, the other from 7 o'clock, with only short bursts in each. Both crashed.

At this time he saw his wingman recovering to the left ahead, and looked back for his second section but could not see them. He did see, however, many "Zekes." He turned onto the closest one and fired a short burst that started smoke and flames, but he did not see it crash, as he was hit at the same time by another "Zeke" firing from ahead. He tried to roll onto this one for a shot, but could not quite make it before the "Zeke" had flown directly in front and over him. His power then failed and his F6F started smoking and flaming badly abaft the engine.

His F6F-3 started smoking badly, then burst into flames. Another "Zeke" made a run on him, hitting his port side many times and breaking loose the instrument panel. He considered trying to put the fire out in the cockpit so he could ditch, but it was beyond control and he prepared to bail out, after giving his position over the radio, which was luckily undamaged. His equipment twice caught on the cockpit enclosure, causing anxious moments, and he left the plane at 2,500ft. Two "Zekes" were circling, so he delayed opening his 'chute until as late as possible. He almost opened his chute too late for upon its opening he made but one swing when he hit the water. He swallowed considerable saltwater while getting disentangled, but he lost it all with no trouble when in his raft.

Throughout the day he fired three Very cartridges at low-flying search planes with no success (the sun was very bright), watched over 350 planes attacking the enemy disposition, stayed out of the sun and dozed. At about 1600 hrs he sighted a friendly surface force and succeeded in getting a "Roger" from a DD [the Fletcher-class destroyer USS *Cotton* (DD-669)] at 9,000 yards with his mirror, and was picked up. He then had the pleasure of watching, from the bridge, the "polishing off" of the enemy carrier he had previously attacked, as well as the sinking of an enemy cruiser in a night action.

After the Battle of Leyte Gulf, Adm Halsey sent three of his four Task Groups back to Ulithi for rest and replenishment after 17 days of almost continuous combat, leaving TG 38.2 off the east coast of Luzon. On October 29, TG 38.2 sent out a fighter sweep, followed by three strikes against the airfields around Clark and Nichols Fields near Manila. Lt William Eder, VF-29 CO, led 16 Hellcats on the early morning fighter sweep, with each F6F carrying a 500lb bomb. These aircraft were accompanied by 16 Hellcats from VF-7 and two from VF-18.

Coming in over Nichols Field, Eder ordered the VF-7 aircraft to attack the airfield, while he took VF-29 to Nielsen Field to the northeast of Nichols. Leaving two divisions as top cover, Eder took his two divisions down on a bombing run – an event that more and more Hellcat pilots were experiencing. VF-29's Aircraft Action Report noted:

An F6F-5 from VF-29 awaits its turn to take off from *Cabot* while an F6F-3 rides the light carrier's solitary catapult. VF-29 replaced VF-31 on board the vessel on October 10, 1944, embarking 18 F6F-5s and three F6F-3s. (80G-286529, RG80, NARA)

Two F6F-5N Hellcats from VF-80 wait to take off from *Ticonderoga* on November 5, with F6F-5s lined up behind them. The unit made its combat debut on this date with a sweep of Manila Bay, VF-80 claiming five Japanese aircraft shot down. Two pilots were lost, however, when, in their eagerness to get at the enemy aircraft, they forgot their air discipline and the advantages of altitude and mutual support. (80G-305244, RG80, NARA)

AA fire at this field was light and of a moderate amount, but three heavy Jap cruisers situated in Manila Bay threw an intense barrage of heavy AA fire at the attacking American fighters. Lt. Eder dove from 11,000ft from the east onto the Field, but his bomb failed to release and had to be jettisoned later. Ens. Eastling's bomb also failed to release and Ens. Combs released his at 2,500ft, having aimed for the hangar south of the runway but failed to make a hit. Lt. Barnes' division followed Lt. Eder's in its dive, releasing at 3,500ft. Lt. Barnes pulled out to observe his bomb hit a barracks building north of the runway. Ens. Murray followed Lt. Barnes in his dive, releasing his bomb at 3,000 ft aimed at a hangar, and he observed it explode close to the side of the building.

Lt(jg) Bishop, about to push over, observed approximately five, apparently undamaged, twin-engined planes parked in the northwest corner of the east-west runway at Nichols Field, and dove on them, releasing his bomb at 2,500ft. On his pullout, he saw the bomb cause a tremendous explosion, with a large sheet of flame and column of black smoke emerge from what apparently was a fuel dump. Two other bombs were also seen to strike in this area, one released by Ens. Balsiger, who dove after Lt(jg) Bishop and aimed his bomb at the same area.

Lt. Eder followed his bombing run with a strafing run directed at a group of planes parked on the runway intersection at the northwest corner of the field, and coordinated with the bombing runs made by planes from USS *Hancock*.

This run was followed by a strafing attack by Lt. Eder, who fired upon a group of planes parked at the northeastern corner of the field and coordinated with a strafing attack undertaken by Lt. Barnes' division and directed at the planes on the northwest runway intersection and at adjacent AA positions. Hits were observed on the planes by each pilot strafing them, but no further damage could be claimed.

Lt. Jacques' flight circling over Nichols Field as high cover at 16,000ft were ordered by the sweep leader to bomb the parked planes at the north side of the field. Lt. Jacques dove on the planes in the revetment area northwest of the runways, gliding down to 12,000ft and nosing over into a step dive from that altitude, releasing at 3,000ft. He was unable to observe the explosion of his bomb due to the fogging over of his windshield. Ens. Wier's bomb hit a large building at the northwest corner of the field and Lt. Thompson and Ens. Van Fleet saw their bombs explode in the area, but were unable to note any damage done.

Following in immediately on the target, Lt. Leslie, leading his division, scored a hit on a medium size building on the west side of the field, while Ens. Bertelson released his bomb and saw it drop on the east-west runway. Lt(jg) Herb was unable to observe the result of his bomb drop. Ens. Stanley Death was not seen again after going into his dive over Nichols Field, and failed to return to USS *Cabot*.

The other fighters of Lt. Jacques' flight pulled out over Manila Bay, passing through the then intense heavy and medium AA fire. On this recovery Lt. Leslie's plane was seen hit by AA, and as the F6F began to trail smoke he pulled around and glided down to make a water landing in Laguna de Bay, a large lake just east of Manila Bay.

While TG 38.2 was sending strikes to the airfields around Manila, the IJNAF sent out small flights from the Tokubetsu Kogekitai (Special Attack Units) to target the American carriers. Ens William Short, with VF-7 embarked in *Hancock*, participated in two CAPs against the attackers, claiming a "Val" and a "Zeke" shot down for his only victories of the war. In the morning patrol Short was leading a section with Lt(jg) Walter Sheen when they were given a vector. VF-7's Aircraft Action Report described the engagement as follows:

Tally-ho was made at 1100 15 miles bearing 180 from the ship, bandits seen were two "Zekes" and a "Val" at 10 o'clock, one mile, 1,500 ft below, on opposite course. The Japs apparently had seen the CAP first as they dropped their belly tanks, and the "Zekes" spread out to about 50 yards to either side of the "Val."

NEW THREAT

On a fighter sweep over the airfields north of Manila on November 6, 1944, Lt Elvin Lindsay, CO of VF-19, Lt Albert Seckel and Lt(jg) Lachlan McLaughlin encountered a Japanese fighter they could not identify. Lindsay shot down one of the new aircraft, only to then be jumped by a second. McLaughlin went after the enemy fighter as it dove past Lindsay, with Seckel joining him in the chase. The Japanese fighter dropped down to 100ft, and Seckel, who was doing 333mph, could not gain on his opponent following the failure of his Hellcat's water injection system. Nevertheless, he kept firing at the Japanese fighter.

McLaughlin's water injection was functioning fine, however, and he overtook Seckel and hit the enemy machine with several bursts before overrunning it. The fighter descended toward the ground, eventually hitting trees and bushes before coming to a halt after losing a wing. Its pilot had by then taken to his parachute, which failed to open fully due to the extremely low altitude at which it had been deployed.

The description the Hellcat pilots gave of their opponents following their return to *Lexington* matched the characteristics of the IJNAF's potent new N1K1-J Shiden fighter, code-named "George".

Ens. W. E. Short started a high-side run on the "Val," while Lt(jg) W. J. Sheen stayed on guard above. As soon as Short was in his run, the "Val" turned left, but Short got in one burst from 1,000ft, high above, 7 o'clock, which drew smoke. He swung down onto the "Val's" tail and kept shooting short bursts as the distance closed, until at about 50ft the Jap blew up.

During this time a "Zeke" got on Short's tail and Sheen made a high-side run at the Jap, who broke off his attack. The second "Zeke" got on Sheen's tail and the one who had just broken off his attack on Short swung around and also got on Sheen's tail. Sheen made hard left-hand turns, but the "Zekes" were turning inside him. In the meantime, Short had climbed back again. Sheen suddenly made a right hand turn towards Short, who opened up with a short burst, out of range. The Japs didn't want to face this opposition so they broke off. One "Zeke" must have swung wide in his turn, as Sheen suddenly saw him coming in from 10 o'clock in a right turn.

Armorers attach warheads to the 5-in. HVARs they will then attach to the underwing rails of a VF-80 F6F-5 in preparation for a strike on Manila during November 1944. This aircraft, chained down to the flightdeck of *Ticonderoga*, is also about to be refueled. (80G-299901, RG80, NARA)

Sheen got in a burst from above, 5 o'clock at 1,500ft, then swung in behind and closed the range, until the "Zeke" caught on fire in the right wing root and was seen to go into the water.

Sheen shot down the second "Zeke" they had encountered, and then he and Short returned to *Hancock*. That afternoon, Short went on another CAP, flying as wingman to VF-7's CO, Lt Cdr Leonard Check. Vectored onto an incoming group of bogies, Check saw a formation of seven "Vals" with an escort of eight "Zekes" above them. He led his division down into the attack, and in the combats that followed claimed four of the "Vals" and a "Zeke" shot down. VF-7's Aircraft Action Report stated:

In the meantime Ens. Short had pulled out above the formation of "Vals" and found himself in the middle of a Zeke–F6F dogfight. During the ensuing battle a "Zeke" suddenly crossed in front of Short and flipped on his back. Short pulled up his nose and fired from 600ft. The "Zeke" burst into flames that enveloped it and went down aflame.

Shortly before the CAP was scheduled to land back on board *Hancock*, the Task Group ran into a solid weather front. The fighters tried to go around the thick bank of cloud, but found it impossible. When the flight was 60 miles away [Ens.] Stockert called and said he had only eight gallons of gasoline left and was going to make a water landing. This was at 1800 and just getting dark. The other planes circled until the plane hit. Lt Cdr Check said that the plane made a normal water landing, but it was too dark on the water to observe whether or not Stockert got into his raft. The

---

1330 hrs, NOVEMBER 5, 1944

WESTERN PACIFIC

1 Ens Joseph Meotti of VF-80, manning a Hellcat on the flightdeck of *Ticonderoga* on standby CAP, is ordered to scramble when kamikaze aircraft are detected. He flies eight to ten miles ahead of the carrier then doubles back, climbing to 4,500ft some 2.5 miles off the port quarter (rear left side), at which point three more Hellcats from VF-80 join up with him in a right echelon.

2 Meotti spots a lone Zero-sen diving out of a cloud at "two o'clock" to him. The IJNAF fighter is making a gentle right turn in the direction of *Ticonderoga*.

3 Meotti, followed by the three other Hellcats, performs a hard right wingover that puts him on the tail of the Zero-sen.

4 Meotti and the three other Hellcats complete their turn, putting them on the tail of the Zero-sen.

5 Meotti opens fire with a three–four second burst from a distance of 1,000ft, hitting the Zero-sen, which continues its dive.

6 Surrounding escort ships target the Zero-sen with anti-aircraft fire. Unperturbed, Meotti alone flies through the barrage to press home his attack on the kamikaze, continuing to fire at the Zero-sen until it wobbles, rolls onto its back and plunges into the water aft of *Ticonderoga*.

7 Meotti climbs back up to altitude in his Hellcat and returns to his CAP station.

FOLLOWING PAGES

position was given to the carrier and two destroyers were despatched to the scene. The search that night and the air-surface search the following day were negative. The remaining VF came into the front and landed aboard in a blinding rain squall.

With the kamikaze threat growing, TF 38 launched a series of strikes against the airfields on Luzon that were the base for the Special Attack Units on November 5–6. Almost 400 Japanese aircraft were claimed to have been destroyed, mostly on the ground. On November 6, Lt Elvin Lindsay, appointed CO of VF-19 just the day before, led 20 Hellcats on a sweep over the airfields around Manila. He took five F6Fs with him up to Clark Field, where they ran into Japanese fighters, including a type they had not seen before. VF-19's Aircraft Action Report noted:

> The six who went up to Clark ran into 15 enemy planes, of which they destroyed 13 without loss to themselves. They were led by Lt. Lindsay, the new squadron commanding officer, who shot down two "Tojos" and one "Oscar." The group was attacked first by five "Oscars," but when our planes turned into them they climbed into the overcast, where Ens. Tatman got onto the tail of a straggler and shot it down in flames. Then singles and pairs of enemy planes came down out of the overcast, and several other enemy planes joined in from the side. All fights took place under the overcast and from 5,000ft down to the ground. A "Tojo" came in on Lt. Lindsay, firing both 7.7 and the two 20mm guns in his wings from above. He was a poor shot, missing, and Lt. Seckel pulled up a bit, centering him with a 60° deflection shot and he burst into flames, crashing. Lt. Seckel comments:
>
> "We encountered 12 to 15 enemy planes, in groups of three to five planes. Lindsay's division and my section kept weaving, covering each other, and by aggressively climbing and turning right into the enemy we kept the initiative, scaring off all but one or two of the planes in the group we attacked. Thus, all of us would gang up on a single plane or two as their pals fled, and we would take turns knocking them down. In a long chase McLaughlin damaged a single-engine fighter of unknown type, and as he pulled out I hit him with a burst and he crashed. This plane was very fast – I was doing 290 knots indicated at 100ft and gaining only a very little. Its wing was a low mid-wing, and the plane resembled a P-47, with a heavy belly below the wing. Carried bombs or tanks under the wings."
>
> Lt. Lindsay added the following observations:
>
> "We all stayed together in excellent fashion and supported each other with no strain. One "Oscar" approached Ens Sassman head-on, then suddenly whipped around and was on Sassman's tail in amazingly short time. He began firing but broke away when he saw my tracers pass him. A few short bursts set his center section afire, and he crashed without bailing out. The "Tojos" pressed their head-on attacks to a very dangerous collision range, where we broke away. One "Tojo," after making such a run on another F6F, tried to pull up sharply into the overcast but burst into flame from my gunfire just before entering the cloud. The sight of a burning "Tojo" spinning out of an overcast is beautiful indeed. I found another "Tojo" (or unidentified plane) in my sights soon after, and a short burst sent him flaming to the ground."

The pilots' description fits the characteristics of the N1K1-J "George," which had been active over the Luzon airfields for some weeks, but apparently without previously being identified as a new type of Japanese fighter.

The plan for air support for the Leyte invasion had called for Gen George Kenny's Fifth Air Force to take over responsibility for air operations from the US Navy at the end of October, but heavy rains on Leyte delayed airfield construction. The Fifth Air Force could only bring up one fighter group, so Gen MacArthur asked that TF 38 and the escort carriers in TG 77.4 remain on station. TF 38 duly continued with strikes against the airfields on Luzon, claiming 129 Japanese aircraft shot down in raids on November 11, 13, 14, 19 and 25. The Japanese attempted to make good these losses by sending aircraft to reinforce the Philippines, but with diminishing returns. Attrition from combat with American carrier fighters and increasing numbers of land-based USAAF fighters steadily reduced Japanese air strength. As a result, the aerial combats during November and December – the last full months of TF 38's participation in the Philippine campaign – never reached the intensity or numbers of enemy aircraft claimed during the October air battles.

One of TF 38's last, best days was on December 14, when TG 38.2 and TG 38.3 sent off several fighter sweeps over the airfields on Luzon as part of TF 38's mission to cover the landings on Mindoro. The newly arrived VF-80 embarked in USS *Ticonderoga* (CV-14) carried out a sweep over the airfields in northern Luzon, where the squadron ran into a large number of Japanese fighters off the east coast of Luzon. The pilots identified the enemy aircraft as "Zekes" and "Oscars," but there is a strong possibility that they ran into Ki-84 "Franks" of 72nd Sentai that were being rushed to the Philippines as reinforcements.

Lt Robert Anderson claimed five fighters shot down to become an "ace in a day," while Lts Patrick Fleming and Richard Cormier claimed four each. Fleming and Anderson were leading their divisions off the coast of Luzon when they saw a group of around 20 aircraft flying ahead of them at the same altitude. VF-80's Aircraft Action Report described the clash that ensued:

They were at first judged to be Japs by the loose, flat formation and by the fact that there were not supposed to be any other friendly aircraft in the area. The F6Fs jettisoned bombs and rockets and closed the formation from astern without trouble, noting 14 "Oscars" and six "Zekes" flying "fat, dumb and happy" at only about 150 knots, weaving slowly back and forth in a sort of scissors maneuver, over a broad front.

It is not known if the Japs were taken by surprise or if, due to poor recognition, they thought our planes friendly. At any rate, our planes came in on a flat pass from astern, using full power and water injection just before the attack, and cut the Jap numerical superiority to about zero. Lts Fleming, Cormier and Anderson each destroyed two Japs, Ens. Beaudry, Hamblin and Smith (showing proper respect for rank) one each, and Ens. Rush and Fraifogl each damaged one.

As the F6Fs were recovering from this first attack, the Japs, who were dispersing both laterally and vertically, were joined by six to nine more "Oscars" coming east from the island. Our VF, again outnumbered and with no altitude advantage, rejoined the fight and a more or less general dogfight resulted. Lt. Fleming and his wingman Ens. Beaudry accounted for three more Japs during the ensuing battle. Ens. Hamblin, accompanied by his wingman, got another and were then forced onto the defensive by three Japanese above them, and which they finally shook by diving for the cloud.

Lt. Cormier got another Jap and then lost his wingman, Ens. Fraifogl, who was forced to take sudden and extreme evasive action to avoid a determined attack on him by another F6F (Ens. Fraifogl is still looking for that "gut" (the last word is an inadequate paraphrase)). Fraifogl then joined Anderson and Rush.

Ens. Rush became separated when they were attacked by three Japanese fighters coming in from different directions. Anderson, with Fraifogl, turned into two and got one, while Rush, turning opposite into the third, got him.

Anderson and Fraifogl, still under attack by other Japs who had a 3,000ft altitude advantage at this point, evaded by diving into a cloud. There, they became separated. Fraifogl came out below the cloud and Anderson pulled up again. There, Anderson was able to burn two of his pursuers in extreme maneuvers. He then joined up on Cormier, and together they chased an "Oscar" until, over the mountains, Cormier polished off the Jap.

The fight by now had moved south to the vicinity of San Fernando and then east. The Japs had either been shot down or dispersed, and the flight with Ens. Fraifogl again joined up, but with Rush missing.

Rush, after getting his Jap, was attacked and forced into evasive action, ending up in the clouds inland, from which he eventually emerged in time to catch the rest of the sweep near the east coast of Luzon. Rush, because of being low on gas and due to impending darkness, landed aboard the *Hornet*. After a pleasant and hospitable interlude, he landed next day on the *Ticonderoga*.

Score for the fracas appears to be 19 Japs confirmed crashed, exploded or burned (not "smoked"), with an indeterminate number damaged. Not a single bullet hole was found in the F6Fs upon returning to the *Ticonderoga*.

After making repairs following a damaging typhoon, the vessels of TF 38 returned to support the landings on Luzon, scheduled for January 9, 1945. The carrier air groups hit Japanese airfields on Luzon, Formosa and in the Ryukyus. On January 9, Adm Nimitz released TF 38 from covering the Luzon invasion and Adm Halsey headed his force toward French Indochina, where he hoped to find two of the IJN battleships that had escaped the Battle of Leyte Gulf.

On one of the last strikes against the airfields on Luzon, a young Naval Aviator from VF-20 had a miraculous escape from death. Ens W. W. Allen was one of ten Hellcats from his unit that was sent out to strike Mabalacat Field, near Clark Field, from veteran carrier USS *Enterprise* (CV-6). Arriving over the airfield, the leader of the formation found no enemy aircraft in the air, so he led the Hellcats down to strafe the field. As the fighters were pulling up from their attack, three "Zekes" jumped them. An F6F pilot fired on one of the enemy fighters, driving him off, but another went after Allen. VF-20's Aircraft Action Report recorded:

One of the other "Zekes" singled out Ens. W. W. Allen, who was off to one side of his teammates, did a split "S" from 1,200ft above and came down on him. Allen attempted to counter the attack by doing a split "S" in the opposite direction, but the "Zeke" caught him in the cockpit with a number of 7.7mm bullets and a 20mm shell. There was a yellow flash and the cockpit filled with smoke. At the same time all pressure on his rudder controls suddenly slackened, leaving him without rudder control. Thinking his plane was on fire, he tried to roll back his hood, but it was jammed, so he attempted to jettison it. When this also failed, he decided he had better try to fly the plane, especially since he was by this time practically on the ground.

He recovered at 500ft all alone northeast of Mabalacat field and headed for the clouds and mountains to the east. Taking stock of his situation, he found that his whole electrical system was out and that his flaps, wheels and hook would not

The Hellcat earned a reputation for being a rugged aircraft. This VF-7 F6F-5 came to grief landing back aboard *Hancock* following a strike on Luzon on December 16, 1944, the battle-damaged fighter splitting in half just behind the cockpit. The flightdeck crew look on as the unharmed pilot is helped out of what remains of his fighter. (80G-259082, RG80, NARA)

LEFT
Ens Stanley Manning returning from one of the December strikes against Luzon. Manning was then serving with VF-20, embarked in *Lexington*, having previously served with VF-11 and VF-7 during the Philippines campaign, he had made claims for Japanese aircraft destroyed with each of the three squadrons in which he had served in 1944. Manning was like most other young Hellcat pilots who claimed a few Japanese aircraft during the Philippine campaign, but never reached ace status. His final tally stood at 2.5 Japanese fighters destroyed. (80G-471764, RG80, NARA)

An F6F-5 of VF-7 starts its take-off run off the flightdeck of *Hancock* for another mission over Luzon in December 1944, the fighter's propeller tips leaving vortex contrails in its wake. VF-7's best day was on October 29 when its pilots claimed 22 aircraft shot down during strikes on Clark Field. (80G-259021, RG80, NARA)

lower. However, he soon found two friendly Hellcats, and after a good bit of frantic gesticulating persuaded them to escort him back to base.

After some faulty navigation, which required retracing their course once, they found TG 38.1 and Allen started making passes at a CV with his wheels up, not daring to lower them with the air bottle for fear that he might have to make a water landing. When the carrier refused to take him aboard in this condition, he picked out a friendly looking DD [the Allen M. Sumner-class destroyer USS *Blue* (DD-744)] and set his plane down a short distance ahead, having by this time rolled his hood back.

The plane remained afloat for 20–30 seconds, giving him plenty of time to climb out, but when he pulled the toggles on his life jacket, nothing happened. He then tried to inflate his life raft, but to his dismay the CO_2 bottle came off. The next 15 minutes were hell, consisting of slow drowning, in spite of the fact that Allen is a good swimmer. He went through all the stages of determination, doubt, panic and relaxation, the last stage being experienced, strangely enough, just after he had grabbed the line thrown by the DD. During the last three to four minutes before being hauled aboard he was entirely submerged, but somehow managed to hang on to the line. By the time they had him aboard he had stopped breathing.

The Medical Officer aboard the DD told him later that it required two hours of artificial respiration, two quarts of blood (plasma) and several injections of Adrenalin to revive him. It was also necessary to remove some pieces of shrapnel from his knee in order to complete the job of restoration. After several days aboard the *Blue* he was transferred to this carrier.

The Philippines campaign saw the longest and most intense period of air combat that the US Navy's carrier aircraft experienced in World War II. During the fighting aircraft embarked in the large and light fleet carriers and the escort carriers claimed 1,622 Japanese aircraft destroyed in the air and a further 1,590 on the ground. Only the victories claimed during the air battles over Okinawa between April and June 1945 come close to these numbers. Loss of carrier aircraft totaled 355 of all types, with around 20 percent being shot down in aerial combat.

The intensity of the action over the Philippines provided many opportunities for veteran and novice pilots alike to make claims for Japanese aircraft destroyed. Some scored victories on multiple occasions, becoming aces (sometimes in a single mission), while many others had just one or perhaps two missions that brought them into contact with Japanese aircraft.

Emblematic of Japan's defeat in the Philippines, a Zero-sen goes down in flames into Subic Bay on December 15, 1944, the fighter having fallen victim to a Hellcat from VF-7, embarked in *Hancock*. American carrier and land-based air power proved overwhelming in the fight to retake the Philippines. Despite throwing heavy reinforcements into the battle, arriving IJNAF and IJAAF units were soon decimated in combat with American fighters. The advent of the kamikaze posed a serious threat to US Navy warships, but the losses they inflicted never prevented the American advance. (NH 95604, Navy History and Heritage Command)

What comes across clearly in the Aircraft Action Reports the squadrons wrote after each mission was the superiority of the F6F over almost all Japanese fighters the Hellcat pilots encountered over the Philippines, and the superiority of their training. While the Hellcat could never completely match the maneuverability of the "Zeke" or the "Oscar," the F6F was always faster, and at high speeds could outperform the Japanese fighters. Many pilots escaped an attack by rapidly diving away. In the main, the Hellcat could take more punishment than Japanese fighters, with the apparent exception of the "Tony" and the later "Frank" and "George." The less-well protected "Zeke," "Oscar" and Japanese carrier and land-based bombers burned readily.

The descriptions of combat in the Aircraft Action Reports bring out the quality of the US Navy's wartime training regime and the tactics taught to the new legions of wartime fighter pilots. There are constant references to fighting as part of a team, to linking up with the first friendly fighter if alone, to making coordinated attacks, flying defensively with mutual support and to the gunnery runs and deflection angles learned in training. Carelessness or neglect could lead to death, as there were, to the very end, very capable Japanese pilots. However, the combination of a superior aircraft and superior tactics and training gave the Hellcat pilots the advantage in the aerial battles over the Philippines.

Cdr David McCampbell (bottom left) and four high-scoring aces from VF-15 pose with the unit's impressive scoreboard towards the end of CAG-15's western Pacific deployment on board *Essex*. Each Naval Aviator is wearing a bandoleer with bullets beneath their life jacket. (US Navy)

AFTERMATH

By the end of 1944, the F6F-5 had almost completely replaced the F6F-3 on board the Essex-class fleet carriers and the smaller Independence-class light carriers. The Hellcat remained the US Navy's predominant carrier fighter through to VJ Day, seeing intensive combat in air strikes against Japan in February–March 1945 and in the battles against the kamikaze over the seas around Okinawa from April to June.

During the fighting over the Philippines, 20 Hellcat pilots claimed five or more victories in a single day, with nine pilots achieving this on October 24, 1944 alone. A further 19 pilots made five or more claims in a single day in the aerial combats over Japan and around Okinawa, demonstrating the Hellcat's dominance over nearly all their Japanese counterparts by this stage of the war. A Hellcat from VF-31, embarked in USS *Belleau Wood* (CVL-24) scored the US Navy's final claim of World War II when Ens Clarence Moore shot down a "Judy" dive-bomber at 1252 hrs on August 15, 1945 – almost an hour after Emperor Hirohito had announced Japan's surrender over Tokyo Radio.

Grumman did develop a more powerful version of the Hellcat in the form of the XF6F-6. Equipped with the Pratt & Whitney R-2800-18W C Series Double Wasp engine, the XF6F-6 made its first flight on July 6, 1944. The C Series Double Wasp was a nearly complete redesign of the R-2800, featuring forged cylinders with significantly greater cooling area and strengthened internal components to cope with higher temperatures and pressures from the increase in horsepower. The R-2800-18W provided 2,100hp for take-off and featured water injection.

In tests the XF6F-6 achieved a maximum speed of 417mph (671km/h) at 21,000ft (6,001m) – a significant improvement over the F6F-5. But using the same engine, the new F4U-4 Corsair demonstrated even better performance than the XF6F-6, with a maximum speed of 446mph (718 km/h) at 26,000ft (7,925m) and an impressive rate of climb of 3,870ft (1,180m) per minute. The US Navy decided to reserve the R-2800-18W for the F4U-4, which began to replace the F4U-1D/FG-1D in land-based US Marine Corps fighter squadrons on Okinawa and carrier-embarked fighter-bomber squadrons from the early spring of 1945.

Waiting in the wings was the Grumman F8F-1 Bearcat, intended as a replacement for the Hellcat on all US Navy carriers. Smaller and lighter than the F6F-5, and powered by the Pratt & Whitney C series R-2800-34W, the Bearcat was faster than the F6F-5 with a top speed of 421mph (677 km/h) and an impressive rate of climb of 4,570 ft (1,393m) per minute, better than the F4U-4. The US Navy placed contracts with Grumman for 2,023 F8F-1s and a second contract with General Motors to build the F8F-1 as the F3M-1. The Bearcat began to replace the F6F-5 with VF-19 in May 1945, but it did not see combat during the war.

Despite the F8F-1's superior performance, replacing the Hellcat with the Bearcat in the midst of operations against Japan, and with an extended supply line stretching from the American West Coast, would have been a daunting task. The Pacific Fleet did not want to disrupt production of the Hellcat at Grumman, then running at a rate of 500 aircraft a month, until the Fast Carrier Task Force had achieved air superiority over Japan. With the expectation that the war against Japan would continue into 1946, the US Navy ordered Grumman not to reduce production of the Hellcat until after August 1945, when the F8F would gradually replace the F6F.

SELECTED SOURCES

Davis, William E., *Sinking the Rising Sun – Dogfighting and Dive Bombing in World War II* (Zenith Press, St Paul, Minnesota, 2007)

Hargreaves, Lt Cdr Everett C., *Son of a Preacher – A Hellcat Ace's Memoirs* (BAC Publishers, Upland, California, 2003)

Hawkins, Capt Arthur Ray, US Navy (Ret), *Angel in the Cockpit* (Arthur Hawkins, Orange Beach, Alabama, 2006)

Jarski, Adam and Waldemar, Pajdosz, *Aircraft Monograph 20 – F6F Hellcat* (AJ Press, Gdansk, Poland, 2006)

Mersky, Peter B., *Whitey – The Story of Rear Admiral E. L. Feightner, A Navy Fighter Ace* (Naval Institute Press, Annapolis, Maryland, 2014)

Meyer, Corwin "Corky" and Ginter, Steve, *Naval Fighters No. 92 – Grumman F6F Hellcat* (Steve Ginter, Simi Valley, CA, 2012)

Morison, Samuel Eliot, *History of United States Naval Operations in World War II: Volume Twelve – Leyte, June 1944-January 1945* (Little, Brown and Company, New York, New York, 1958)

Morison, Samuel Eliot, *History of United States Naval Operations in World War II: Volume Thirteen – The Liberation of the Philippines: Luzon, Mindanao, The Visayas 1944-1945* (Little, Brown and Company, New York, New York, 1958)

Reynolds, Clark G., *The Fast Carriers – The Forging of an Air Navy* (McGraw-Hill Book Company, New York, New York, 1968)

Tillman, Barrett, *Hellcat – The F6F in World War II* (Naval Institute Press, Annapolis, Maryland, 1979)

Tillman, Barrett, *Osprey Aircraft of the Aces 10 – Hellcat Aces of World War II* (Osprey Publishing, Oxford, 1996)

Tillman, Barrett, *U.S. Navy Fighter Squadrons in World War II* (Specialty Press, North Branch, Minnesota, 1997)

Winters, Capt T. Hugh, USN (Ret.), *Skipper – Confessions of a Fighter Squadron Commander 1943-1944* (Champlin Fighter Museum Press, Mesa, Arizona, 1985)

Wooldridge, E. T., Ed, *Carrier Warfare in the Pacific – An Oral History Collection* (Smithsonian Institution Press, Washington, D. C., 1993)

INDEX

Note: page locators in **bold** refer to illustrations, captions and plates.